# What People Are Saying about *Power Your Organization's Fundraising...*

*Joanne Oppelt provides concise, succinct, practical tools for nonprofit leaders to develop the relationships needed to succeed financially. She provides a unique perspective, using a broad range of resource development principles, to help nonprofits function more efficiently and effectively.*

**Amy Eisenstein, CFRE**
**Author, Speaker, Consultant, Coach**
**Tri Point Fundraising**

*Power Your Organization's Fundraising should be in every fundraiser's library—the volunteer, the novice, and the seasoned professional. It is overflowing with wisdom, expressed in a reader-friendly way, with fascinating fundraising experiences. Joanne Oppelt conveys realistic situations and practical solutions with compassion and a deep understanding of the special relationship between the donor and the charity professional.*

**Michael Discroll, CFRE**
**Vice President of Advancement, Don Bosco Preparatory School**

*Defining a partner as "any person or group of people who is interested in the success of your organization," Joanne Oppelt uses this concept to highlight the importance of understanding your organization's strategic plan, finances, brand, and culture to ensure financial success. If you're interested in increasing your agency's bottom line by expanding its reach,* Power Your Organization's Fundraising *gives you a great road map.*

**Lucinda Mercer, CFRE**
**L M Consulting**
**Grant Writer, Financial Development Consultant, CASA Advocate**

*In my many years as a director for nonprofit organizations, I have never run across a more informative fundraising book. I am recommending this book to every new and experienced fundraiser and grant writer out there who needs a push in the right direction. Her samples of a budget outline are excellent and great tools to help one get a sense of where to begin. Joanne Oppelt's new book,* Power Your Organization's Fundraising: How the Partnership Paradigm Will Change Everything, *is a must-read.*

**Dana Sharpe, Project Director, HR Director**
**Plainfield Community Outreach Inc.**

*This book is an insightful look at the many kinds of partnerships that impact a nonprofit organization. Covering the basics, such as identifying prospective partners—including those who are hiding in plain sight—building strong relationships, mutual goal setting with organizational partners, and good stewardship, this book also delves into what to do when it's time to "break up" with a professional partner. It is an interesting and informative must-read for nonprofit professionals.*

**Beth Blakey**
**President, ReWrite Consulting**

# Power
## Your Organization's Fundraising

### How the Partnership Paradigm Will Change Everything

Joanne Oppelt, MHA, GPC

Vauxhall Branch Library
123 Hilton Avenue
Vauxhall, N.J. 07088

**Power Your Organization's Fundraising: How the Partnership Paradigm Will Change Everything**

One of the **In the Trenches**™ series

Published by
CharityChannel Press, an imprint of CharityChannel LLC
30021 Tomas, Suite 300
Rancho Santa Margarita, CA 92688-2128 USA

charitychannel.com

Copyright © 2013 by CharityChannel Press, an imprint of CharityChannel LLC

All rights reserved. No part of this book shall be reproduced, stored in a retrieval system, or transmitted by any means, electronic, mechanical, photocopying, recording, or otherwise, without written permission from the publisher. No patent liability is assumed with respect to the use of the information contained herein. This publication contains the opinions and ideas of its author. It is intended to provide helpful and informative material on the subject matter covered. It is sold with the understanding that the author and publisher are not engaged in rendering professional services in the book. If the reader requires personal assistance or advice, a competent professional should be consulted. The author and publisher specifically disclaim any responsibility for any liability, loss, or risk, personal or otherwise, that is incurred as a consequence, directly or indirectly, of the use and application of any of the contents of this book. Although every precaution has been taken in the preparation of this book, the publisher and author assume no responsibility for errors or omissions. No liability is assumed for damages resulting from the use of information contained herein.

In the Trenches, In the Trenches logo, and book design are trademarks of CharityChannel Press, an imprint of CharityChannel LLC.

ISBN Print Book: 978-1-938077-36-4 | ISBN eBook: 978-1-938077-33-3

Library of Congress Control Number: 2013943620

13 12 11 10 9 8 7 6 5 4 3 2 1

Printed in the United States of America

This and most CharityChannel Press books are available at special quantity discounts for bulk purchases for sales promotions, premiums, fundraising, or educational use. For information, contact CharityChannel Press, 30021 Tomas, Suite 300, Rancho Santa Margarita, CA 92688-2128 USA. +1 949-589-5938

## Publisher's Acknowledgments

This book was produced by a team dedicated to excellence; please send us your feedback to editors@charitychannel.com.

We first wish to acknowledge the tens of thousands of peers who call charitychannel.com their online professional home. Your enthusiastic support for the **In the Trenches™** series is the wind in our sails.

Members of the team who produced this book include:

### *Editors*

**Acquisitions Editor:** Linda Lysakowski

**Comprehensive Editor:** Kathy Wright

**Copy Editor:** Marcie McGuire

### *Production*

**In the Trenches Series Design:** Deborah Perdue

**Layout Editor:** Jill McLain

### *Administrative*

**CharityChannel LLC:** Stephen Nill, CEO

**Marketing and Public Relations:** John Millen

# About the Author

Joanne Oppelt has been improving organizational bottom lines since 1993. Currently Executive Director at CONTACT We Care in New Jersey, Joanne manages day-to-day agency operations, develops budgets, increases net revenues, and oversees organizational marketing and resource development efforts. She is also an adjunct professor at Kean University, where she teaches courses in nonprofit management and fund development.

As Development Director at Community Access Unlimited (CAU) for nine years, Joanne personally raised more than $9.3 million through government, corporate, foundation, and individual support, increasing agency annual operating revenues by more than $1.75 million. She also generated hundreds of thousands of dollars in cost reductions by negotiating strategic vendor relationships. In addition, Joanne created the agency corporate marketing materials and instituted the CAU Community Network.

During her tenure at Prevent Child Abuse-New Jersey, Joanne oversaw a $1.2 million U.S. Department of Education grant. She formed a statewide Parental Assistance Advisory Committee, bringing together groups with competing agendas in a common goal. She also garnered national and state recognition of the organization as the NJ Parents As Teachers State Coordinating Agency.

While at the March of Dimes Central Jersey Chapter, Joanne facilitated the funding allocation process through the volunteer Health Professionals Advisory Committee. She also facilitated the volunteer Community Health Education Committee, where she implemented professional education conferences and increased volunteer participation in the Babies and You Speakers Bureau by 200 percent.

Joanne's other books include *Moving Up to Executive Director: Lessons Learned from My First 365 Days, Succeed in Your Nonprofit Funding Partnerships: Analyzing Their Costs and Benefits*, and *Confessions of a Successful Grants Writer: A Complete Guide to Discovering and Obtaining Funding.* Joanne holds a Bachelor of Arts in Education from Bethany University in Santa Cruz, California, and a Master of Health Administration from Wilkes University in Wilkes-Barre, Pennsylvania.

She lives in New Jersey with her husband, Rick.

# Dedication

This book is dedicated to my children, Sarah Ann, Michelle Elizabeth, and Timothy Richard, who inspire me to bloom in full.

# Author's Acknowledgments

First of all, thanks to my publisher, Stephen Nill. Steve has spent countless hours with me perfecting the final product that is this book. He spent many hours on the phone with me, patiently listening to me and guiding me with his hand of friendship. Steve is an invaluable resource to me and a wonderful confidante. I appreciate all Steve does.

I thank my employers, CONTACT We Care, Community Access Unlimited, Prevent Child Abuse-New Jersey, March of Dimes Central Jersey Chapter, and Maternal and Family Health Services. They have all given me opportunities to explore and develop my talents and to learn new skills. Without their investments in me, I would not be where I am today.

I also thank my students, who make me think through the answers I give to the questions they ask. They help me to clarify my thoughts and be clear in my communications.

Thank you to my manuscript reviewers: my father, Nate Heuberger; Beth Blakey; Jeffrey Feldman; and C.J. Jones.

My friends and my network keep me sane. Especially Leslie, Dottie, Joyce, Denise, Priscilla, and Carol. I thank them for being there for me.

A special thanks goes to my forever friend, C.J. Jones. C.J. has been there for me through thick and thin. She has watched me change and grow. She has always encouraged me. To her, I will always be grateful.

I thank my children, Sarah, Michelle, and Tim, who grew up with my workaholism and still love me.

Mostly, I thank my husband, Rick. I am a better person because Rick is in my life.

To all of you, I am truly blessed to have you in my life.

# Contents

Foreword . . . . . . . . . . . . . . . . . . . . . . . . . . . . . . . . . . . . . . . . . . . . . xvii

Introduction. . . . . . . . . . . . . . . . . . . . . . . . . . . . . . . . . . . . . . . . . . . xix

**Chapter One**
Identifying Partners. . . . . . . . . . . . . . . . . . . . . . . . . . . . . . . . . . . . 1

**Chapter Two**
Relationship Building . . . . . . . . . . . . . . . . . . . . . . . . . . . . . . . . . 17

**Chapter Three**
Increasing Income: A Spectrum . . . . . . . . . . . . . . . . . . . . . . . . . . . 27

**Chapter Four**
Reaching Your Potential Partners . . . . . . . . . . . . . . . . . . . . . . . . . 39

**Chapter Five**
The Larger Context . . . . . . . . . . . . . . . . . . . . . . . . . . . . . . . . . . . 55

**Chapter Six**
Financial Considerations. . . . . . . . . . . . . . . . . . . . . . . . . . . . . . . 71

**Chapter Seven**
Ensuring Maximum Profit . . . . . . . . . . . . . . . . . . . . . . . . . . . . . . 89

**Chapter Eight**
Making the Deal . . . . . . . . . . . . . . . . . . . . . . . . . . . . . . . . . . . . . 99

**Chapter Nine**
Maintaining the Partnership. . . . . . . . . . . . . . . . . . . . . . . . . . . . 111

Conclusion. . . . . . . . . . . . . . . . . . . . . . . . . . . . . . . . . . . . . . . . . 119

### Appendix A
Association of Fundraising Professionals Code of Ethical Principles and Standards . . . . . . . . . . . . . . . . . . . . . . . . . . . . . . . . . . . 121

### Appendix B
Grant Professionals Association Code of Ethics . . . . . . . . . . . . . . . 127

### Appendix C
Glossary . . . . . . . . . . . . . . . . . . . . . . . . . . . . . . . . . . . . . . . . . . . . . . . . 131

### Appendix D
Recommended Reading. . . . . . . . . . . . . . . . . . . . . . . . . . . . . . . . . . . 135

### Index . . . . . . . . . . . . . . . . . . . . . . . . . . . . . . . . . . . . . . . . . . . . . . . . . . . 139

# Summary of Chapters

**Chapter One: Identifying Potential Partners.** In Chapter One I cover how to strategically approach potential partners with specific outcomes in mind. Topics include the role of the strategic plan, how to build off existing partnerships, partnering with organizations with similar goals, and partnering with organizations with similar markets.

**Chapter Two: Relationship Building.** Chapter Two is about how to help the donor feel an important part of your organization's success. In this chapter I cover the role of active listening, the feedback loop, and building trust. The chapter also provides ways to acknowledge and validate your donors.

**Chapter Three: Increasing Income: A Spectrum.** In Chapter Three I focus on the many ways to increase the bottom line for your organization. Cash donations, in-kind contributions, and the use of volunteers are a few of the better-known income sources in the development field. Others include improving your organization's brand, increasing your customer bases, and reducing your business costs.

**Chapter Four: Reaching Your Potential Partners.** Individual, foundation, corporate, and government funding partners have different values, different motivations, and different perspectives. In Chapter Four I talk about meeting your funding partners where they are. I cover the importance of matching missions, developing your brand, knowing your organization's financial and market performance indicators, and thoroughly researching the labyrinth of legislation involved in governmental funding.

**Chapter Five: The Larger Context.** Chapter Five is all about how culture, the economy, politics, regulatory bodies, and the media affect the environment in which your organization operates. I cover ways you can work to ease the negative effects of your environment and positively influence those who control that environment.

**Chapter Six: Financial Considerations.** In Chapter Six I lay a framework for analyzing potential partnerships in financial terms. The chapter covers how to calculate your direct and indirect costs, opportunity costs, and net income. I also talk about market-based and profit-based pricing strategies.

**Chapter Seven: Ensuring Maximum Profit.** Positive net income can tell you if you are coming out ahead of the game, but there are other financial calculations that can tell you how to allocate your resources for maximum profit. In Chapter Seven I focus on return on investment. I also talk about cash flow and cash-flow considerations.

**Chapter Eight: Making the Deal.** In Chapter Eight I talk about the factors that come together in actually making the deal. The chapter covers how to formulate overarching goals and the basis on which they are formed. I also talk about the importance of fair process as well as fair outcome. The chapter ends by addressing ethical considerations and the importance of having an exit strategy.

**Chapter Nine: Maintaining the Partnership.** If you want continuing results from your partnerships, they need to be maintained. In Chapter Nine, I talk about the importance of reporting returns on partners' investments and relating those returns to mission. I also cover the importance of keeping your partners informed amidst a changing environment. In addition, I explore the importance of following up on your promises and periodically reassessing the costs and benefits of your partnerships.

# Foreword

Every once in a while I pick up a book and say, "Gosh, I wish I had written this." *Power Your Organization's Fundraising: How the Partnership Paradigm Will Change Everything* is one of those rare books. I loved the title as soon as Joanne told me about it. Wouldn't we all love to "power up" our fundraising?

But, as you read this book, you'll find out it does not focus on the techniques of raising money—hundreds of books out there do that. It focuses on something more important than that. It focuses on a concept near and dear to my heart.

I have been in fundraising for more than twenty-five years and have been fortunate enough to have had some wise mentors, taken advantage of a lot of top-notch educational opportunities, and read a lot of great books written by the "gurus" in this field. As I have matured in my own career, I have also been fortunate to learn from some of the people I have mentored; I have gained valuable insights from participants in my training classes and have benefitted from the experience of authoring, co-authoring, editing, and co-editing more than a dozen books. But throughout my career I always remembered one of the earliest lessons I learned: that fundraising isn't learning about how to raise money; it is more about the three key words in fundraising—*relationships, relationships, relationships.*

And that is what this book is about.

Joanne's treatment of how to build relationships with *all* of your partners is a tremendous contribution to the world of fundraising. As you delve into **Chapter One**, I think you will find your organization has more partners than you might realize you have. We so often neglect to focus on our own "family"—our boards, our staff, our vendors, our volunteers; instead we focus only on foundations, corporations, and individual donors. This book might open your eyes to another whole world of internal partners who can be your greatest allies. At the same time, it can help you expand your reach to your external partners—the media, government, foundations, businesses, and individuals in your community.

I encourage you to have your pencil and highlighter by your side as you read this book. You will want to make copious notes to refer back to throughout your fundraising career. In fact, I would suggest you read **Chapter One** thoroughly and beside each category of partners mentioned write down how much you raised from each of these constituencies last year. At the end of this year, go back to your notes and see how much more you've raised after learning about how to communicate more effectively, form wise partnerships, and treat your partners fairly as Joanne recommends. I think you will find in the end that you have indeed shifted your own paradigm and built a more powerful fundraising program.

**Linda Lysakowski, ACFRE**
President
Linda Lysakowski LLC

# Introduction

**Raising Money: It's All About Partnerships**

Together, everyone achieves more. This maxim certainly holds true in the world of fundraising.

Usually, when we think about fundraising, we think in terms of the types of fundraising we do: capital campaigns, planned giving, major gifts, special events, direct mail, proposal writing, corporate contributions, government contracts, social networking, newsletters, and the like. We focus on the vehicles we use to raise the funds. We read books, attend workshops, and participate in webinars that focus specifically on the field of fund development that we are trying to learn. We usually begin our careers mastering one form of fund development and then another. We become experts in our field by mastering them all.

I am a successful fundraiser, yet I am not expert in all the available vehicles that exist to raise money. Rather, I am successful because I know and understand how to develop partnerships.

Raising money is about forming partnerships: partnerships with people and groups of people who can add to your organization's bottom line. I use the term "partnership" very broadly. I define a partner as any person or group of people who is interested in the success of your organization. Partners can be not only collaborators, but also staff, board members, volunteers, donors, and vendors. They usually have one or more goals similar to yours. Sometimes, though, partnerships are based on common market bases and your partner seems quite different from you. Extremely different. So different, in fact, that it seems you have nothing in common with each other. In these cases, you might have to dig very deep for commonalities.

Defining partnerships in such a broad way allows you to accept all kinds of contributions that help your organization's bottom line. Contributions that go beyond money. There are an almost infinite number of ways that a potential partner—that is, anyone interested in the success of your organization—can give to your organization. Limiting the contribution to a monetary one, in my mind, is reaping only a fraction of what can be gained.

Partnerships help your organization further its impact. Furthering your impact only helps your organization become more financially stable. Strong organizations that make substantial impact with leveraged resources are attractive to all kinds of funding partners. Success breeds success.

This book approaches fund development from a new perspective. It introduces an innovative paradigm to use in designing your development plan, as opposed to a more traditional approach. Putting the transformative partnership paradigm into practice will lay a strong foundation for sustainable funding long into the future.

This book will tell you how to broaden your base of partners by understanding and meeting both your needs and theirs. You will learn about good communication and relationship-building skills. You will explore the role of values and how connecting on the basis of values improves the strength of your partnerships. You will understand different types of revenue streams and the tools needed to accept and receipt them. You will also find out about the larger partnership context and how to influence the larger environment such as the effects of culture, the economy, political systems, and the media.

I then talk about financial and profit considerations, with plenty of examples of how to predict whether your partnership will be profitable or not. The topic then turns to actually making the deal, both through fair process and fair outcome. The book ends by briefly discussing how to maintain partnerships once they are formed.

Each chapter begins with an overview of its main concepts followed by a brief introduction. Throughout the chapter, you will find sidebars that add detail to the narrative, give hints on applying the principle being discussed, or relate real-life experiences in dealing with the pertinent subject matter. The chapter is briefly concluded and ends with practical suggestions for real-world application drawn from that chapter's subject matter.

I am a successful partnership builder. In this book I share the lessons I have learned over the years and the strategies that have worked for me. If you and your organization embrace the following concepts, your agency will be able to raise lots of money and build a solid future. Good luck in your search for funding.

# Chapter One

## Identifying Partners

**IN THIS CHAPTER**

- The importance of the strategic plan
- Leveraging existing partnerships
- Organizations with similar goals
- Organizations with similar markets

In the traditional sense, our organizational partners are our collaborators, the other organizations that work with us in meeting our mission. Usually we think of our partners as groups similar to us in some way, often organizations that serve the same group we are serving, such as at-risk youth or people who are homeless. And sometimes our partners are organizations that are part of a larger group we are part of, like an association of nonprofits.

But partnerships can extend beyond common client groups or business structures. They can include relationships with donors, volunteers, employees, and vendors. Basically, a partner can be defined as anyone who interacts with your organization and is interested in its success. But partnerships can go even beyond this. They can expand to include other groups that share organizational market bases whose contributions go beyond the immediate donations a partner might make. By opening up your paradigm of who your partners are and what your partnerships can offer, you can reap rewards that will help sustain your organization well into the future.

> A partner can be defined as anyone who interacts with your organization and is interested in its success.
>
>  finition

Identifying potential partners is not just approaching other organizations or people who have a lot of money or clout with the hope that they feel like sharing it with you. It means approaching others in a meaningful, planned way with specific outcomes in mind.

You and your organization need to remain faithful to your mission, first and foremost. It is your mission that defines your organization and gives it identity. You must identify other partners that will contribute to your organization's fulfilling its mission. To do that, you've got to know not only your needs, but also the needs of your potential partners.

## The Strategic Plan

The first step in identifying partners is taking stock of organizational goals. The types of partnerships you pursue depend on what you want to do and how you decide to get there. Deciding on organizational goals and objectives is part of the strategic planning process. Strategic planning is a board and executive director responsibility. But usually department heads or program managers are responsible for action plans to make sure that these goals are operationalized, that is, put into operation. Meeting some goals might require partnering with others. But note that the partnerships you form should support organizational goals. A successful partnership doesn't exist just because you like each other, one of you is famous, or one of you has money. Whatever partnership you are looking to form, that partnership must support your organizational goals in order to be a win for your organization. Successful partnerships are based on shared goals.

A good strategic plan not only outlines organizational goals, but also identifies organizational values. Your organization's values tell the world why you do what you do and why you do it in the way you do it. Your partners will partly be determined by these same values. For example, if you value healthy living, you will probably not approach tobacco companies or related entities as partners. Instead, you will look at organizations that also value health like a state Department of Health, a local hospital, or a gym franchise. If your organization values transparency and therefore makes its financial statements available on its website, you might also want to look for partners who make their financial statements easily accessible to the public. In addition to shared goals, successful partnerships can be based on shared values.

A good strategic plan also defines the context in which the organization operates.

- ◆ What are the organization's strengths and weaknesses?
- ◆ What does the organization do well?
- ◆ Who are the organization's constituencies?
- ◆ What are the constituencies' strengths and weaknesses?
- ◆ What do you bring to the table when considering a partnership?
- ◆ What can you deliver?
- ◆ Does the potential partner agency help you grow your strengths or compensate for your weaknesses?
- ◆ What does the agency bring to the table?

## Existing Partners

The first place to look for new partners is through your existing partners. No matter how new or small your organization, you always have existing partnerships.

### *Trustees*

An organization's strongest volunteer partnership is with its board of trustees. Board members

> An agency's strategic plan tells you a lot about that organization and is well worth the read. A thorough strategic plan is crucial to keeping everyone on the same map going toward the same destination. A thorough strategic planning process includes representatives from all the agency's major constituencies, taking into account their values and perspectives and getting them invested into the organization's success. That is why it is important to regularly update your strategic plan—to keep up-to-date with changing market conditions and to keep all key stakeholders vested in the success of your organization.
>
>  practical tip

believe in the work and are highly invested in the organization. They should be your organization's strongest allies and promoters. Board members can help you recruit other volunteers. Board members might have to be trained in how to do the recruiting and what opportunities are available in your organization, but they can be a valuable resource. Recruiting volunteers can help reduce program and operating expenses and open even more doors for you. Think of your board members as a networking vehicle for you.

In their role as the agency's strongest advocates, board members should also be taking the lead in supporting the organization financially. Your board sets an example to others. They should be lead givers. Not that they should or can give the highest amounts, but they should be the *first* to give or pledge to your organization, and *each* of them should contribute. They take the lead in governing the organization; they should also take the lead in financially supporting it. It is a very strong statement to other potential donors that an agency has 100 percent board giving. In fact, 100 percent board giving is required by more and more foundation contributors.

And just as board members engage in recruiting volunteers, they should also recruit other donors. Most people, board members included, are afraid to fundraise. People generally think of "making the ask" when they think of fundraising. In fact, though, the actual "ask" is only about 10 percent of the fundraising process. Board members can, and should, do a host of other things besides asking for contributions. They can make introductions to other business professionals for you. They can open up their home for a small soiree. They can invite a friend or colleague to one of your events. They can call on previous donors and just thank them. A good fundraiser should teach board members what else needs to be done and how they can do it. It is up to the fundraiser to know the strengths and interests of board members and use those for the best possible outcome. Board members want to contribute. They just need to be taught how.

> Board members, like all volunteers, will have their own strengths and abilities and preferences for how they want to be involved. Make sure you have plenty of options available to them.
>
>  practical tip

There are numerous resources on the market to engage board members in fundraising. For a few of them, I recommend starting with BoardSource, which can be found on the web at www.boardsource.com.

## *Employees*

An often-overlooked partnership is the one you have with employees. If managed correctly, employees are some of your best agency promoters. Employees spend a majority of their time with your organization. Employees are responsible for carrying out your organization's mission;

> At one agency in which I worked, we wanted to increase revenues to the general fund to which individual staff members were already contributing. One of the major sources of funding for our general fund was an annual walk-a-thon. We started a campaign to teach staff how to ask for donations to our walk. We started the "10 for 10" concept: each staff person asked ten people for ten dollars each. Soon, the amount of per-person contributions was higher than ever.
>
> Then some of the staff suggested that they be given the option to hold small events to help them raise money instead of making a direct ask. Soon departments were banding together and holding small events. The fundraising coordinator helped the staff advertise the events and took care of the record keeping; the staff was responsible for all the logistics.
>
> The results exceeded our expectations. Teams competed to see which one could raise the most money. The team that raised the most money got an agency-paid pizza party. Individuals also competed. The individual who raised the most money got an extra paid day off. Events were held year round. Team and individual standings were mentioned during every department-head and full-staff meeting. Soon, people were vying not only for the prizes, but also for the bragging rights. Revenues tripled.
>
> Now, staff members look forward to coming up with the most creative participatory ideas that they can. Coordinating the events is used as team- and leadership-building activities. It has become part of the culture there to integrate fundraising with mission and staff development.
>
>

they understand what the agency is all about from a front-line perspective. They can tell you the real-life stories of how individuals and families are positively impacted by what your organization does. If tapped into properly, they can be one of the best public-relations vehicles your agency has.

Positive relationships with employees are crucial to promoting the good will and brand of your agency. If they feel they are contributing and valued, good employees recommend and encourage other good potential employees. Employees who are satisfied in their jobs and feel good about what they do are also a good donor base. Employees who feel the organization is supporting them are often most happy to support the organization. They become vested in the mission. Just as 100 percent board giving makes a strong credible statement, so does 100 percent employee giving.

### *Vendors*

Vendors are also vested in your organization, though not nearly as much as board members and employees, and for different reasons. They might or might not care about your mission, but they do care about your business. They want to see you succeed and thrive. Perhaps you will become a larger customer. Perhaps you will refer business to them. Perhaps your employees or volunteers will take advantage of their products. At the very least, they want to make a good impression on you so you will come back again and again as a repeat customer. Your success is their success. What a motivator!

To tap into the vendor market, you need to think like a businessperson. You need to present your agency as a profitable, successful business as opposed to a nonprofit, do-good agency. You are fostering business-to-business relationships rather than provider-to-client or organization-to-donor relationships. When your organization presents itself as a provider or a charitable cause, your mission drives you. When you present your organization as a business, market forces and economics drive you.

My success in expanding organizational business partnerships has been in large part because I have been aware of the environment within which businesses operate and the values that drive them. It takes work to do that, though. It means going to chamber of commerce meetings and events. It means getting involved in my local business and industry association. It means reading the newspaper, especially the business section. It means subscribing to business media such as magazines, websites, blogs, and other publications. It means understanding and accepting a very different point of view than the one I might currently hold. My job is not to change our partners and make them more like me or to change me to be more like them. My job instead is to find ways we can work together toward common goals. My first step is to understand their environment, their struggles, their challenges, and their viewpoints.

The greatest need for any consumer-based business in a market-based economy is customers. For-profit companies invest a lot of money in trying to attract potential customers. Customers are the base of their revenue streams. Without customers, businesses cease to exist.

In the vendor relationship, your organization is the customer. Your organization contributes to the vendor's revenue stream. The more revenue your organization contributes, the more important a customer your agency is. The question then becomes, especially for small organizations, how to increase the vendor's potential customer base.

This is why sponsorship works so well. If you are holding an event in which the vendor's potential customer base participates, the vendor will want to market its services to that base. Don't think only in terms of your organization's special-events participants; think of what you have to offer as a total organization: your volunteer base, employee base, and other nonprofit organizations you collaborate with. For example, your accounting firm will probably find organizations such as yours attractive potential customers, and it might be worth a monetary investment on its part to reach those customers. In this case, think about any events that you hold that could bring your nonprofit collaborators together. Perhaps a training session at which the vendor can present? Align the event with other marketing opportunities you have available.

How many ways do you have to recognize vendors? Signage at an event? Recognition in an event program? Recognition on an event invitation? Promotional materials in your goody bags? What about website opportunities? Annual report listings? Mention at staff meetings, particularly if you have a large staff? Mention at volunteer trainings or events, especially if you have a large volunteer base? What do your vendors now pay for exposure like this? How much would they be willing to contribute to advertising with you?

But this approach only works if you understand your vendors' markets. Who are their customers? Are any of your constituencies a potential customer base for them? You need to know your own markets as well as theirs. Perhaps a business will find it worthwhile to give to you out of their marketing budget as well as out of their charitable gifts budget.

Not all vendors are in it only for the increased customer base, however. Remember that vendor companies are run by people. Most vendors, like most people, have a need to make a difference in the world and feel like their contribution is valued. Your job is to know your agency's vendors and what drives them. They might become donors because they believe in your mission.

Vendors might give back in the form of monetary donations, in-kind donations, or reductions in price. All three are valuable kinds of contributions. I talk more about the value of different types of contributions in **Chapter Three**.

Sometimes the monetary gain is small compared to what else you might gain from vendors. For example, your vendors will know your business practices better than most of your other constituencies. They can help develop and promote your brand. They can testify to your solidity as a well-managed entity. You can ask them to tell others about your strong business practices. You might even be able to use a quote from them in your public-relations materials.

> **watch out!**
>
> A market-based relationship is the basis of cause marketing, through which for-profit companies engage in and contribute to nonprofit organizations for the purpose of increasing market share. Canisters at the cash register and corporate sponsorships are relatively simple, tried-and-true cause-marketing activities. Cause-marketing agreements can be quite complicated, however, requiring formal, legal, complex contracts. Cause marketing works well for many organizations. However, if you do engage in cause-marketing partnerships, be aware of the tax laws regulating the types of revenue a nonprofit must declare as unrelated business income. Cause-marketing activities sometimes straddle the fine line between mission-related and business-related income.

*Clients*

Clients, especially former clients, should always be looked at as potential partners. These are the people who have tried your product or received your organization's services and can testify to the quality of what you offer. They can give personal testimony and credible stories of how your agency's products or services have impacted their lives. Clients are extremely important partners and need to be cultivated.

Educational institutions are masters at forming partnerships with former clients. For example, colleges and universities foster alumni societies, activities, and events. Students give a significant time investment to post-secondary educational endeavors. The assumption is that this investment has paid off and they are grateful to their institutions for their return on investment. Students also transition through an important life stage during their college years: they build strong, often lifelong, relationships during this time. People generally have fond memories of their time at their alma mater. Educational institutions use these feelings of goodwill and nostalgia to their advantage. A significant portion of most college and university fundraising is through alumni giving.

But what if yours is a human-services agency with a low-income clientele? How can you convert these clients to partners? Well, they can provide testimonials for you. If you have the proper releases, you can feature them in your newsletter, annual report, or website. They can tell their stories at donor-cultivation events. If they are seeking to give back or looking for skill-building opportunities, they can volunteer for you. They can testify at a legislative hearing or work a "get-out-the-vote" drive. There are many ways besides giving money that a client can contribute. I will talk more about volunteering in **Chapter Three**.

Everyone, no matter what their abilities, skills, or income level, can give back. It might take some creative thinking on your part to involve all of your partners in a meaningful way, but it can be done.

*Volunteers and Donors*

If you are looking to increase your volunteer or donor base, the best people to partner with are your current donors and volunteers. They are invested in your mission. They are engaged with your organization. They think well enough of your agency to give of their time, talent, or treasure. They can be your best allies in expanding your development efforts.

> One agency I worked for supported people with developmental disabilities, most of whom had come from institutional care. One of the very real ways the clients partnered with the agency was by going back into the institutions and talking to the current residents about what it was like to live in the community. This partnership helped empower our clients and boosted their confidence, and at the same time furthered the agency's mission. When the state began a concerted effort to move people from institutional to community care, our client volunteers were already experienced and our agency was already known for the quality services it delivered in the community.
>
>  **stories from the real world**

As discussed earlier, your lead volunteers and donors are ideally the members of your board. If you need somewhere to start growing either a volunteer or donor base, start with your board. Form volunteer committees that have board representation and board backing. Your board might form a development committee and have it take the lead in reaching out to other organizational volunteers and donors. Send invitations from board members asking others to join your committees and be a part of your events.

Even if you don't have a development committee, highlight how important all your volunteers and donors are in what they do. Be specific about how your volunteers and donors have contributed to the organization and what impact that has made on people's lives. Make giving to your organization a highly rewarding experience for others. Motivate them. Get them excited about what they are doing.

If your volunteers and donors feel fulfilled when they contribute to your organization, they will keep doing it. They will also spread the word about their positive experiences with your organization and how great your agency is. They will most likely be happy to help you recruit others like them so that their friends can have the same fulfilling experience. People like to recommend good deals to other people. Plan to have the reward you offer appear to be a good deal for those who volunteer or donate.

Tapping into your volunteer and donor bases requires good volunteer management and donor-retention techniques. There are numerous books available regarding these topics. I highly recommend *Recruiting and Training Fundraising Volunteers* by Linda Lysakowski and *The Volunteer Management Handbook: Leadership Strategies for Success* (Second Edition), edited by Tracy Connor.

**Organizations with Similar Goals**

One of the easiest ways to identify potential partners is to look at agencies with missions similar to yours. Of course that will include other nonprofit provider agencies similar to yours. This is what professional associations are all about. For example, the Child Welfare League of America brings together organizations that work with children and youth; the American Hospital Association brings together hospitals; the National Assembly of State Art Agencies brings together state arts organizations; and the Center for Nonprofits brings together the nonprofit community. These associations work because the agencies affiliated with them have similar goals: They want to better the plight of children and youth, improve the hospital industry, bring the arts to more and more people, or tackle issues relating specifically to nonprofits. And, as a large group, the associations generally offer benefits that are more efficiently and effectively attained through a group, rather than an individual effort. Such as hosting conferences. Or influencing policy.

Some funders partner with you on the basis of similar missions. Furthering its mission is what a foundation's giving is all about. A foundation will give to a nonprofit organization because it believes the nonprofit has the capability and resources necessary to carry out what that foundation wants to accomplish.

Foundation boards are interested in making an impact in the world regarding the issues they care about. The agencies they invest in are only vehicles they use to make that impact. With foundations, it's all about matching missions and how well you carry out that mission.

> Foundations do not give *to* organizations as much as they give *through* organizations.

I once created a community network of area businesses in order to strengthen our agency's business-to-business relationships and, at the same time, further the quality of life for people we served. I got the buy-in from my executive director and was off recruiting area businesses from our lists of vendors and funders. The participation rate was smaller than I had hoped for, but still significant.

I saw this as a network of potential donors and volunteers and cultivated it as such. In recognition of the demanding schedules of business executives, the group only met twice a year, and I provided breakfast. Before each meeting I gathered data on the business operations of our agency so that my audience could relate to me on its terms. The executive director's participation, as head of our organization, was crucial. I invited him and the executive staff of the other agencies to attend. Each meeting started and ended on time; we never went beyond the allotted time. At each meeting I allowed plenty of time for networking, presented a PowerPoint presentation, and had a couple of clients present personal testimonies of the impact the agency was making. I ended the meeting with a call to either support our next fundraising event, donate to our Hope Chest (household items for clients just setting up their own apartments), or help in an upcoming advocacy campaign. At the following meeting, I would update the group members on how their efforts had made an impact on people's lives and contributed to the group's goals.

And you know what? It worked! The committee really got behind the Hope Chest donations. I even had one company offer to feature needed items with a short blurb about the agency periodically in its customer newsletter. And when the time came for input to the federal government about the HUD strategic plan, network members gave it. Uniting people around a common goal and mission had worked. Our clients' lives were enhanced by donations from group members, and our agency benefited from the ensuing HUD policy changes. Just as important, we had stronger documentable partnerships with the community, something our funders loved.

Sometimes you are asking your partners to further an agenda that specifically affects how your agency delivers services or the population your agency supports. You see this all the time with advocacy campaigns. Your partners in this case will be anybody affiliated with you who is interested in strengthening your impact: board members, volunteers, employees, clients, donors, and sometimes vendors.

Look, also, to for-profit service providers that you might not usually think of: employers, landlords, medical providers, local businesses. If your clients' welfare is affected, how will that affect their consumption of community goods and services, i.e., the local economy? How big is your agency's network? How well are you known in the community? What type of impact are you making?

## Organizations with Similar Markets

One of the biggest differences between for-profit and nonprofit organizations is the complexity of multiple constituencies the nonprofit organization faces. Who are your organization's markets? What are their needs, desires, and values? Do you share any of your markets with anybody else? Partnerships sometimes start between organizations because of shared constituencies and constituency needs.

Corporations invest a lot of money into reaching potential customers. They invest heavily in market research and knowing the needs, desires, and values of their customers. They spend gobs and gobs of money on trying to get the attention of potential customers and increasing the company's market share. Bigger market share means bigger profits and greater company worth.

So companies will pay a nonprofit to expand the exposure of the company or company's products if that nonprofit has access to the company's potential customer base. Savvy nonprofits have been forging these kinds of relationships for years. The trick to getting this piece of the revenue stream is in thoroughly understanding your nonprofit's multiple market bases.

The first place to start is your client base. What do your clients have that someone else values? Do they go to a gym? Do they shop at a particular store or supermarket? Do they pay utility bills? Do they bank? Are they looking for housing? Do they vote? All the things that people do in their daily lives are potential touch points for a business or organization that provides goods or services in these areas. Any way that you can provide name recognition or product promotion is financially worth *something* to *somebody*.

The same questions and principles can be applied to your other constituencies: your volunteers, donors, employees, and networks. Who are they as a group? What are their needs? Who do they like to affiliate themselves with? What is important to them?

It is often very difficult for those of us who are mission driven to think of relationships with clients, volunteers, donors, and networks in business terms. These are, after all, people who have come to us because they need what we have to offer or believe in our mission. These are not people we should take advantage of by partnering with some greedy corporation trying to make even more money than they already do.

My philosophy is that my clients, donors, volunteers, employees, and networks have multiple needs, not just the ones met through their relationship with me. I find no conflict of interest in exposing them to goods and services that will meet those other needs. Especially from those businesses that support my cause.

And I gain so much more than money from these cause-marketing relationships. I have a documentable relationship with the community. I am leveraging my funding with other community partners. I am gaining visibility for my cause among a public I probably wouldn't otherwise reach. I am able to better meet my mission because of the added funding. I am also better able to position myself with other funders and donors, which might lead to even more funding partners. To me, this is a win-win relationship for all involved: my clients, donors, volunteers, employees, and networks get exposed to goods or services they might need; the partnering company reaches more potential customers; and I get increased funding, organizational visibility, better positioning among my funders, and more mission impact. I can live with that!

You have a lot to gain by embarking on these cause-marketing relationships. But you *must* be careful. Everything, every detail, must be carefully laid out for the relationship to work. When you partner with a for-profit company, you are probably partnering with an organization with a very different culture, language, and set of expectations. Don't assume anything. Don't assume you understand each other just because you use the same words. Those words may have very different meanings to them than to you. Take the time to be meticulous and to lay everything out. *Everything.*

Proper planning prevents poor performance. Know the needs, wants, and desires of your potential partners before you meet with them. Know what they want to get out of the partnership with you. Don't assume that just because you value something, they do too. Know why a relationship with you is important to them and how it meets their needs. It's not all about you, your organization, or your clients. It's about them too.

## To Recap

- ◆ Base your partnerships on the direction provided in the organizational strategic plan.

- ◆ Utilize board members as your strongest volunteer allies and lead donors.

- ◆ Explore employees, vendors, and clients as potential pools from which to develop strong partnerships.

- ◆ Use existing volunteers and donors to enhance expansion.

- ◆ Enhance your development efforts by partnering with organizations with similar goals.

- ◆ Explore partnership possibilities with organizations with similar markets.

# Chapter Two

## Relationship Building

### IN THIS CHAPTER

- Communication and the feedback loop
- The importance of listening
- Making the emotional connection
- Building trust

Partnerships are based on relationships. In creating a partnership, you must define how the involved parties will relate to one another and what each can offer the other. Some partnerships are more formal than others. Partnerships relating to money are more emotional than most people think. In our culture, money, in many ways, represents our worth and the worth of our hard work. Self-worth deals with values and emotions. When we talk about raising money, we must be aware of just how personal and emotional the topic might be. It is important that we understand our partners' motivations and reservations. The first step in getting to know a potential partner is to listen to what they have to say.

### Communication Theory

Basic communication theory tells us that in every interpersonal interaction there is a message to be communicated by a sender to a receiver. The sender encodes a message, picks a form of communication, and sends the message. A receiver then receives the message and decodes it. Dialogue occurs when the receiver, in turn, sends a message back to the original sender. Pretty basic stuff.

But often the communication ends up in a situation such as this: "I know you think you understand what I said, but I'm not sure that what you heard is what I meant." Happens all the time.

Misunderstanding happens because encoding and decoding are heavily influenced by background, such as one's culture, education, or profession. Corporate cultures vary from business to business, and nonprofit cultures tend to vary greatly from for-profit ones. For example, appropriate business attire might mean suit and tie in a corporate environment but only slacks and a button shirt in a nonprofit.

What is said in one culture might not mean the same as in another. Especially when you take into account that communication is only 7 percent verbal. Thirty-eight percent is communicated through tone of voice and 55 percent through nonverbal gestures. Even when two people are from the same corporate culture, they might have different education levels and different vocabularies. Often, people in the same corporate culture come from different professions, each with its own jargon and ideas of what is important. There are many ways that "what you heard is not what I meant" can happen.

> One of my favorite examples of not hearing what was meant comes from my personal life. One day at the mall, without cell phones in hand, my husband and I decided to do our own shopping and meet up at the entrance of one of our favorite restaurants at the appointed time. The appointed time came, and both of us were at the restaurant entrance. Yet we each waited alone for half an hour, each getting more and more infuriated by the minute. The problem was not that we weren't there on time; the problem was not that we didn't stay in one place and wait for the other to arrive. The problem was that we were each at separate entrances. We had both heard to meet at the entrance but failed to clarify exactly what we meant. We each heard correctly, but we did not mean the same thing.
>
> **stories from the real world**

In addition to the differences in encoding and decoding, noise surrounding the message can also distort it. People are people, and everyone has lives that extend beyond the communication at hand. If your daughter is sick and in the hospital, you are probably not going to pay attention to what I have to say about work-related topics as much as you usually do. Or if you just had a big fight with your spouse, you might be a little more sensitive to corrective feedback than if that fight had not happened. Life happens. Thousands of things distract us.

So how do I know that I heard what you meant? And how do you know I heard what you meant? The answer is simple. And yet, most communication goes awry because this simple solution is not implemented. And it is hard for many people to implement the solution even though it's an easy and simple thing to do.

What is the solution? It's the feedback loop. The feedback loop is the basis of you getting to know your partner and setting the tone for establishing the parameters as to how that partnership will be conducted.

Simply put, a feedback loop occurs when a message has been transmitted and the receiver tells the sender what was heard and asks if that is what the sender intended. Simple. But we sometimes find it hard to do. Many people feel foolish asking if they understood the other person correctly. Somehow they think they should know what the other person meant, or they don't want to take the time, or they fear they will look dumb if they ask. But really, there isn't any other way to make sure you're both on the same page. It's even more important when more than two of you are involved in one interaction.

To establish an effective partnership you must first establish effective communication. And the first step to establishing effective communication is to use the feedback loop.

The feedback loop is important to practice not only so you can make sure that you and another person understand each other; it is also important because of the nonverbal messages it sends. People want and need to be validated. Listening and feeding back what they're saying is one way to do that. Taking the time to make sure you understand what someone else says tells that person that what they have to say is important to you. It shows them respect. It shows that understanding the other person's needs is something that you want to take time doing. It tells the other person that you might be a good potential partner.

> One time a donor made a major gift to the organization I was working for. We decided on an amount and a timetable for making payments. He wanted the donation charged to a credit card and asked me to notify him of each payment to the card. I agreed, and he made the first installment.
>
> When the time came to make the second payment, I, according to our agreement, made the payment and then gave him an immediate call telling him that I had made the charge.
>
> He blew up. He had wanted me to notify him *before* I made the charge to his card, not after. Since he had given me the card number and we had agreed on a timeline, I assumed he meant to go ahead and charge the card. He thought that if I had the card number, it would save him from having to give it to me each time. In his mind, our agreement was that I would notify him before I made the charge, in case any unforeseen life happenings had occurred that would prevent him from fulfilling his next installment.
>
> Luckily, I did not lose the donor. But I could have saved us both a lot of aggravation if I had used the feedback loop until we both completely understood the process we would follow for each installment.
>
> **stories from the real world**

People have lots of things to do in this busy world. Respect the time that they are giving you. Respect that they are using up precious moments of their lives to interact with you. Whether they say good things or bad things, things you agree with or things you don't, the fact that people give of their time and effort means they believe whatever they have to communicate to you is important. Your job is to be a sleuth and find out what is motivating them to interact with you. You can only do that by listening to what they say and feeding back to them what you think you heard.

## The Importance of Listening

The most important skill in being able to feed back what you hear is the ability to listen—actively listen. Active listening is the first step in getting to know a potential partner. And it is the way to get people interested in what you have to offer. Yes, that's right. Getting people invested in your product, service, or organization starts with listening to their needs and interests, not in describing what you have for them. Your initial job is not to promote your service or organization; it is to find out what your potential partner's needs are. You can't do that if you're talking. You need to listen first.

In your role as fundraiser, volunteer recruiter, contract negotiator, or organizational collaborator, whatever the partnership is, you want to find out all about your potential partner's goals, values, and motivations. You can only do that by listening to them. People generally like to talk about

> At one organization for which I worked, I was responsible for the agency's public-relations activities but given almost no budget to implement them. (Sound familiar?) So I called around to the local newspapers to research their coverage areas and the costs to advertise. I also wanted to know about the probability of press coverage for agency press releases. So I called and talked to account representatives, trying to see what kind of deals I could get.
>
> When I got to one newspaper, I noticed that the account rep took particular interest in what I was trying to do. So I fed back to her what I perceived as her interest and asked her if my perceptions were correct. She confirmed they were. I followed up by asking her if she had any personal experience with the issue I was trying to address, and she told me she had. She then went on to tell me about how one of her close family members was personally affected by the issue and how, in turn, the issue had impacted the entire family. She was keenly interested in doing anything she could to alleviate the issue.
>
> Guess what? I not only got a great advertising rate and good press coverage; I got an excellent advocate for the cause. This woman was always on the forefront of any of my advocacy campaigns. She even took time from her job to come to some of our community meetings. All because I started with listening to her and feeding back what I heard and giving her the opportunity to talk about what was important to her.

**stories from the real world**

what's important to them. Let them. Get them talking by asking questions. And then listen to what they have to say. What they say might surprise and delight you.

Listen, listen, listen. Most conversations with potential partners should involve about 80 percent listening. People will not be able to tell you what motivates them if you are doing most of the talking. You will miss what they have to say and what's important to them if you are thinking about the next thing you are going to say. Listen. Actively listen. Listening is imperative to success.

## Making the Connection

According to modern social theorists and linguists, most communication is nonverbal. The words that we say make up only about 7 percent of our actual communication. The tone of our voice makes up another 38 percent, and body language the remaining 55 percent. If you can pick up on the nonverbal cues, you will have a window into the soul.

I bring up nonverbal language because that is where most of the indicators about a person's feelings will be. Most of us, particularly in professional settings, don't talk about our feelings. Some of us never do. But we do have them, and we do express them, whether verbally or nonverbally. Feelings are where we make emotional connections. And emotional connections are our strongest connections.

Emotional connections are important because that's how we relate to one another as human beings. Success in forming partnerships, especially partnerships with donors and volunteers, depends in large part on how well you can make those emotional connections. People want to feel that they are contributing to an endeavor that will make a positive difference in the world. They want to feel a part of something bigger than themselves. They want to be accepted and appreciated for what they have to give. They want validation, to feel that they matter to someone.

If you want to establish a strong connection with someone, provide feedback on the person's words and feelings. Validate the other person by identifying the feeling and feeding it back, no matter what that feeling is. This doesn't mean you need to mirror the feeling or respond to it, just recognize it and feed it back verbally. By doing so, you will validate that person's feelings; the person will feel more accepted by you. If people feel accepted, they feel safe and will probably risk revealing more about themselves.

Getting people to talk to you openly like this is a major coup because it enables you to find out about their motivations for wanting to enter into a partnership with you and what their reservations are in doing so. It is important that you not skip this step or assume you know why people are doing the things they are doing. Although you might have a pretty good guess, you never know until you confirm it. And once you do know it to be true, you periodically need to re-confirm what you know because people and circumstances change.

For example, people tend to volunteer for causes with which they have some type of personal connection. Do you know your volunteers' stories? Are they friends with one of your staff? Did they volunteer for a similar organization and have a good experience? Has there been someone in their immediate family affected positively or negatively by the issue your organization is addressing? Do their friends volunteer at your organization? Was your organization recommended by someone they respect, such as a minister, priest, or rabbi?

> I once had a major donor who was angry that I didn't interact with him enough. His solution was to call the executive director and complain that I wasn't doing my job. Rather than defending myself when time came to resolve the issue, I asked about his feelings. I used phrases such as "it sounds like you are angry" and "it sounds as if you don't feel appreciated" to confirm what he was trying to tell me. This gave him an opportunity to clarify his feelings. I did not mirror his anger, just articulated and acknowledged it. As a result, he felt understood. His anger subsided, and we were able to reach an amicable solution to his wanting to be more involved.
>
> **stories from the real world**

The same principles apply to donors. Knowing their stories, why people choose to give of their precious resources to your organization, helps you to meet them where they are, develop a strong emotional connection, and create a long-lasting partnership.

Recruiting new donors is much more expensive than retaining current donors. It is estimated to cost six times more to acquire a new donor as opposed to keeping one. So, it is in your best interest to develop strong, emotional connections with your partners and keep up those connections.

## Building Trust

> **observation**
>
> In the United States, people are very generous in their charitable giving. In 2011, donors in the United States gave about $298.42 billion to nonprofit causes, about 2 percent of GDP. (GDP, or gross domestic product, is the total financial value of all the goods and services produced in a year.)
>
> Retaining these donors, however, is not easy. Fundraisers in the United States are notoriously bad at keeping donors for any length of time. As of this writing, the current first-year donor retention rate is just over 29 percent. That means that for every ten new donors in a given year, seven of them will not give in the second year.

Identifying and validating feelings is often the first step in building a trusting partnership. If people feel you understand them, they are more likely to trust you. If people feel you accept them as they are, they will feel safe with you and trust you.

Of course, there are many other elements to a trusting relationship as well. You need to say what you're going to do and do what you said. You need to be reliable and dependable. People need to know what to expect from you. Don't promise something that you or your organization can't deliver. Be authentic. Act with integrity.

You need to tell the truth, too: the truth about your cause, your organization, and yourself. Nothing destroys trust as much as a lie or a half-truth. Don't overinflate your cause's impact or importance. Don't fudge your organization's results. Be honest. Always tell the truth.

When entering a potential partnership, start with where *the potential partner* is, not where you are. Use the partner's language, which you learn through active listening. Let your partners know you understand what they are saying about what they can and can't do. Respect their limits.

Don't ask your partners to change who they are, their perspectives, or their feelings. Accept each partner in totality. Point out and build on strengths. Be safe for the partner. Be open. If your partner is angry over something, feedback the feelings but don't respond in kind. Your partner needs to know you can handle it when things go wrong. Be a safe haven for the partner.

> **practical tip**
> 
> I cannot overestimate how important establishing and maintaining trust is to a partnership. Without trust that you will at least abide by the terms of the partnership, you have nothing. Your partners must also trust that you will keep them informed when you can't meet your end of the bargain.

All partnerships are about relationships. How someone allocates resources—time, talent or treasure—is a value decision. People have lots of options in choosing partners. They will more likely choose a partner who understands and validates them over someone or some organization that treats them as one of a crowd.

If you want to stand out from the pack, to raise more revenue than you ever imagined, work on making your donors, volunteers, and other partners feel that their contributions are among the most important contributions to your success. Let them know how important they are to you and your success. Accept them for who they are and what they have to give. Validate them. Be authentic with them. Let them know they are a part of something worthy that is bigger than themselves. Meet their needs. Listen to them and know them. Whatever work you do in gaining their trust and making them feel good about their existence will pay off in spades. I guarantee it.

## To Recap

- ◆ Practice active listening.
- ◆ Use the feedback loop.
- ◆ Make an emotional connection.
- ◆ Be authentic.
- ◆ Validate your partners' contributions.

# Chapter Three

## Increasing Income: A Spectrum

**IN THIS CHAPTER**

- Options for cash donations
- Accepting in-kind contributions
- The value of volunteers
- Raising your brand
- Increasing your number of customers
- Reducing costs

It is the mission that defines who your organization is and what it does. But money enables your organization to carry out that mission. Without adequate resources, your organization will be extremely limited in the kind of impact it can make. Mission is what builds your organizational machine; money is what makes it work.

There are two ways to increase an organization's income: increased revenues and decreased expenses. For the purposes of this book, I am including both in my definition of raising money.

### Cash

Let's talk about cash first. Cash is usually what we think of when we think of raising money.

Cash, especially cash not designated for a specific purpose, is highly sought after. In the nonprofit world, we call these gifts unrestricted donations. This cash can be used where your organization deems it most necessary. This type of cash pays the rent and utilities, the marketing expenses, the human resource and accounting personnel salaries, and any other overhead expense you can think of. Often, foundation and governmental funding is restricted to the operation of a certain program or cannot be used for general operating expenses. However, your organization must still incur and pay for operating costs to remain viable.

> **watch out!**
>
> Just because your organization might raise lots of unrestricted cash does not mean that it can spend it on high overhead expenses or administrative salaries. Today, there are too many accountability mechanisms in place for you to risk having inordinately high overhead costs. The recent changes in the 990, which almost every nonprofit must file and make public, are great examples.

Cash donations are also the easiest to measure. We set a goal, we ask for donations, and we either meet or don't meet that goal. We ask for donations through check, credit cards, or cash. We make it easy to make a cash donation: direct-mail appeals, website donation buttons, corporate sponsorships, ticket sales, auctions, raffles, product sales, investment income, wills, annuities, giving groups. The list can be endless.

Many of us believe that the more avenues you have for a person to make a cash donation, the better off you are. In many ways, this is true. You want to give your donors choices in how they can give and how they feel most comfortable supporting the organization financially. You don't have choices just to have choices, though. For optimal results, match your type of ask to the needs of your donors.

For example, I have donors who just don't want to give to or participate in my annual gala. They do not see the value of paying for a ticket when a third of their donation will go toward paying for their meal. I have other donors who plan their annual giving specifically around the gala. They see the gala as a worthwhile social event where our organization can introduce our mission to many community stakeholders.

It is a waste of my time and resources to try to convince my supporters in the first group to change their mind and support the gala in any way, even though the event is important to the organization's revenue mix. The gala just isn't their thing. I'm much better off courting them in other ways. Hence, for those donors who don't support my gala, I engage them in conversation and actively listen to them. I find out about their values and how they would like to make a significant contribution to the agency. Then I make an ask that fits their needs and values.

So listen to your potential donors and find out what best meets their needs. Then match your allocation of resources to the types of giving avenues you can promote among your various constituencies.

**In-Kind Contributions**

In-kind contributions are noncash contributions. For budgeting and tracking purposes, in-kind donations can be given a monetary value, but no actual cash exchanges hands.

In-kind contributions can be almost any type of noncash contribution. For example, one organization might provide office space free of charge for another organization. A business might donate office furniture or computers to your nonprofit. Individuals might donate used clothes to organizations that then sell the clothing and use the proceeds to further their mission. You might donate old cell phones to a domestic violence shelter. All are in-kind contributions. In-kind contributions can take many forms.

In-kind contributions are sometimes easier for donors to give than cash contributions. For example, if you gain or lose weight, you might have

> You have options in the ways people can give to your organization not just for the sake of having options, but to meet the needs of your financial partners. Unless you are a big organization with lots of resources at your disposal, you will be making choices about what kind of marketing you will do around your mission and the options for donors to give to that mission. You cannot do everything, especially if you are a small organization with a limited budget. Make sure that the donor strategies you decide to invest in fit the needs of your donors.
>
> 👍 practical tip

clothes that are good enough to still wear but don't fit anymore. If you want someone else to benefit from still usable clothes, the easiest thing to do might be to donate them. Plus, you might be able to get a tax break for your donation as an in-kind contribution. In the same vein, if a company is moving or upgrading or downgrading office space, its old furniture and computers might still be usable. It might be in the company's best interest to try to find an organization it can donate to rather than trashing the items. Corporate donations to good causes of any kind help a company's reputation in the community and might also give the company a tax break.

Tax-deductibility, although not usually a primary motivator, is key to increasing used-good donations as opposed to having potential contributors throw them away. Many businesses seek out nonprofits and donate furniture and computers to them because of the tax advantage it gives the corporation. I know that I, as an individual, have given my used clothing to Goodwill, the Salvation Army, and Lupus Foundation because I know that my contribution will not only help someone else, but also because I can receive tax deductions for my donations.

> **watch out!**
> When your organization accepts in-kind donations, be aware of the IRS requirements for accepting, valuing, and receipting them. You will need this information for your organization's financial reporting. Your donors will need this information in order to take appropriate tax deductions.

Sometimes people give in-kind contributions rather than cash because they know their contribution will be used in a specific way. For example, a parent organization might donate books to a classroom because they want their children to have ready access to plenty of reading materials. Some donors might find a contribution more real for them when they give an actual, tangible book as opposed to a check. Some donors might feel more secure that their donations will actually be used for classroom reading if they give actual books or subscriptions, as opposed to risking having the cash redirected somewhere else if times get tough. Some donors might have really been touched by certain books as children and want to share their heartfelt experiences by creating greater access to those reading materials for others.

Sometimes in-kind donations are significant in terms of value and maintenance, such as a house, or boat, or timeshare. Before you accept these kinds of donations, you need to know if you can use them. For example, at one organization I worked for, we used donated houses for the people we served. Housing was a major thrust of the organization. A donated house was a good thing and worth the rehabilitation and maintenance costs.

At another organization, a very generous donor gave us a timeshare. We were ecstatic, having something we could use as an auction item year after year. That is, until timeshares became a dime a dozen and we weren't getting enough in auction bids to cover our maintenance fees. What seemed a wonderful gift early on had become a white elephant. Then we were faced with the touchy situation of selling off the gift while not offending the donor.

Smart organizations have gift acceptance policies for just such situations. Gift acceptance policies state what you will and won't accept under what conditions and what will happen to the gift. For example, will your organization accept a gift of a valuable painting if someone bequeaths it to you? Would you keep it or sell it? If you keep it, can you afford the insurance on it? If you sell it, can you afford the marketing costs associated with reaching art enthusiasts? If there is a time lapse between when you accept it and when you sell it, can you afford the storage costs?

Gift acceptance policies work for lower-valued items, too, such as used clothes, furniture, or other items. Do you have the staff or volunteer labor to sort through it all and see what can be salvaged and what must be thrown away? Do you have the staff, volunteers, or funds to be able to

> **stories from the real world**
>
> When I worked at one organization, we had what we called the Hope Chest program where we put together baskets of items young people would need to set up house in their first apartment. People could give cash or in-kind donations. It always surprised me how often donors to this particular program chose to donate the actual dishes or silverware or bathmats for the basket as opposed to cash to buy the items. It paid off to have choices available to people who wanted to contribute.

restore or fix items so they can be sellable? Do you have the space to store them while being refurbished? Do you have the space to show the items? Do you have the staff to show the donated item to prospective buyers or end users?

> **practical tip**
>
> It is often hard to say no to someone who is motivated to give you something that person thinks will have value to you. A gift acceptance policy lets you say no graciously. In addition, a good policy tells the donor that you are a savvy organization that has done its homework and that has the best interests of the people you serve at heart.

When looking at in-kind contributions, clearly define your policies and procedures. Do an analysis of both the costs and benefits of accepting the different types of donations you might be offered. You might be surprised—that high-value gift you are so excited about might end up costing you more money than it is worth. I talk more about financial considerations in **Chapter Six**.

## Volunteers

Good volunteers are worth their weight in gold. Many organizations exist only because of volunteer-driven initiatives and programs.

In the simplest definition, volunteers involved in operations are unpaid staff. They perform services vital to an agency's operations, yet they are not paid for their services. Most people cannot afford to volunteer full-time hours; hence organizations get mostly part-time unpaid staff. This means there might be many more volunteers contributing to the operation of an agency than paid staff. Volunteers contribute to lower organizational operating expenses and increased organizational capacity.

Notice how I refer to volunteers as unpaid staff, with emphasis on the word "staff." My point here is that to get the most contribution from your volunteers, you need to view them and treat them like professional staff. Provide job descriptions. Interview them. Train them. Give them meaningful work. Give them incentives for good performance. Evaluate them and give them feedback. Do everything you would do if those volunteers were paid professionals. Value their work in the same manner as paid staff. You will reap rewards beyond your wildest dreams.

Many resources in the marketplace deal in depth with recruiting and retaining volunteers. Two I suggest are *The Volunteer Management Handbook: Leadership Strategies for Success* (Second Edition) by Tracy Connor and *Recruiting and Training Fundraising Volunteers* by Linda Lysakowski.

> **observation**
>
> Donated volunteer time can be calculated as revenue and reported as such. The value of volunteer time contributions is governed by IRS and state regulations.

## Increased Brand Value

What is a brand and why is it important? A brand, simply put, is your organization's reputation. Your organization's mission tells everyone how you impact the world. Your organization's brand tells everyone how well you deliver on your promises. People want to be a successful part of something bigger than themselves. Your brand, in part, tells them if they can do that through your organization.

The first thing many people think of when they think of an organization's brand is its logo. A logo is an important representation of your brand, but it is *not* your brand. Your logo may make a visual impact, but the *total* impact is your brand. Many things help determine your brand, including the following:

- ◆ How well do your employees serve your clients?
- ◆ What do your clients think?
- ◆ How quickly does your organization respond to requests for information?
- ◆ How transparent are you?
- ◆ How honest and forthright is your organization in how it allocates revenues and expenses?
- ◆ How quickly do you thank your partners for their contributions?
- ◆ How much credit for your success do you give your partners?

All of these things and much more determine your brand. Anything that you can do to improve your overall image, your brand, is well worth the time, effort, and expense you put into it.

An organization with a good brand has tremendous credibility in the marketplace. In the nonprofit world, you have multiple markets in which to attract donors. You will have an easier time attracting good board members and loyal donors if people know you are trustworthy and reliable in meeting your mission and doing what you say you will do. Your agency will attract paid staff and volunteers who want to work for you if you have a reputation as a good place to work. Vendors will be more likely to negotiate with you if you have credibility in meeting your obligations and you have a reputation for good business practices. In short, an organization with a favorable brand will attract more partners and more funding than one with a poor brand. Paying attention to your brand pays off.

> **observation**
>
> In the for-profit world, especially among large companies, an organization's brand has monetary value and appears on the balance sheet as a financial asset.

Many books in the marketplace deal with nonprofit marketing and branding. I highly suggest Katya Andresen's book *Robin Hood Marketing: Stealing Corporate Savvy to Sell Just Causes*. I also recommend *Attracting the Attention Your Cause Deserves* by Joseph Barbato, *Cause Marketing for Nonprofits: Partner for Purpose, Passion and Profits* by Jocelyne Daw, and *Brandraising: How Nonprofits Raise Visibility and Money Through Smart Communications* by Sarah Durham.

## More Customers

Increases in gross revenues are usually a reflection of increases in volume, increases in price, or a combination of the two. The more products or services that you sell, the more gross revenue you take in. Same with price—the higher the price at the same volume, the more revenue you'll generate. In this section, I will deal with increased volume only. I will talk about pricing strategies in **Chapter Six**.

One way to increase revenues is to increase the size of your customer bases. Because a nonprofit deals with multiple constituencies from multiple markets, a nonprofit has multiple customer bases.

The first customer base people usually think of is that of end users, the people who benefit from the services provided. If you are a fee-for-service agency, then increasing the number of clients you serve will increase your gross revenues. If you count on third-party donors to pay for the services your organization delivers, an increased client base indicates growth, and growth suggests fulfilling a greater amount of unmet need. Growth also indicates client satisfaction with your services. These are things that help you help your donors feel a successful part of something bigger than your organization. And having donors feel their contribution makes an impact makes it easier to cultivate new donors.

So how do you increase your client base? Usually, that's not a problem. In nonprofit work, there is usually more need to go around than resources to meet it. So you end up with waiting lists. Waiting lists, or numbers of unserved clients, are important. Waiting lists show demand for services. Unmet demand implies inherent quality of product or service. The logic is that your services are worth waiting for.

Unmet need and quality of service are two bases in which you compete for another customer base—funders. Donors are interested in impacting a particular community need. You must give them evidence that a need exists in your community and show them that you are the best organization to meet that need.

That is why you promote your brand. A positive brand, with supporting evidence, makes it a lot easier to convince donors that you are one of the best alternatives out there. Once a donor is interested in you as a chosen alternative, your first priority is to establish a trusting relationship. Your job at that point is not only to convince the donor that you *can* do the job, but also that you *will*.

Note that I am only talking about gross revenues here. I have not taken into account any costs associated with increasing a customer base. Sometimes, when you take into account your organization's costs, you actually lose money when you increase gross revenues. I will talk about costs and their analyses in **Chapter Six**.

## Cost Reductions

The last type of income I will talk about is cost reductions. The two ways to increase net income are through increases in revenues or through decreases in expenses. Cost reductions are not revenues; they represent a decrease in expenses.

There is always a cost to doing business. There are rent or mortgage payments, utility payments, salaries and wages, costs to run payroll, account fees, loan fees, and interest on loans. You have computer programs and software licenses to purchase, office supplies to buy, printing costs to produce your outreach materials, and mailing costs to get them to your prospective audiences. The list goes on and on. Any cost reduction helps improve your organization's financial performance and can increase the amount of resources your organization has available to meet its mission.

> **stories from the real world**
>
> Cost reductions can be significant to an organization's bottom line. I once negotiated an $800,000 refinancing deal at a below-market interest rate that saved the organization about $250,000 over the life of the loan.

Cost reductions in long-term partnerships, that is, those that decrease price significantly below market rate, generally require having some sort of well-established, trusting relationships in place, because the loss in revenue to the long-term vendor is significant. These vendors will want something from you that makes their sacrifice worth it. For philanthropic vendors, knowing that they are helping the cause in a significant way might be enough. Other vendors might want something else. Listen to them to find out what is important to them, what their motivations are, and what they expect in return. Know what you're getting your organization into before you sign on the dotted line.

I talk about negotiating partner relationships in **Chapter Eight**.

There are many ways to increase the bottom line for your organization. Cash donations, in-kind contributions, and the use of volunteers are a few of the better-known revenue streams in the development field. Others include improving your organization's brand, increasing your customer bases, and reducing your business costs.

## To Recap

- Implement donation channels that meet your donors' needs and match your overall organizational marketing strategy.

- Know the guidelines for accepting, valuing, and receipting in-kind contributions.

- Create a gift acceptance policy.

- Treat your volunteers as valuable members of your professional staff.

- Improve your brand.

- Consider increasing your customer bases.

- Reduce business costs where you can.

# Chapter Four

## Reaching Your Potential Partners

**IN THIS CHAPTER**

- People give to other people who ask them
- The importance of matching missions
- The significance of a good brand
- Organizational financial and market performance
- The intricacies of governmental funding

One of the basic human needs we all have is to be acknowledged and validated. We want to do a good job at work and have our bosses praise us when we fulfill or exceed expectations. We want our spouse and children to tell us they love us. We want our friends to socialize with us. There are many ways we reach out and connect to others and ask them to tell us that we are important to them. So it is with our partners, although the connection between the two parties might vary on how personal the connection is or how personally it is expressed.

## Individuals

Approximately 80 percent of all charitable giving in the United States is through individuals. The exact percentages vary from year to year, but are pretty consistently around 80 percent or so. Paying attention to what motivates individuals to give pays off big.

There are two rules that guide me when I ask for money from individuals: (1) people give to other people, and (2) people give because they're asked. People giving to people speaks to the relationship you've been able to develop with them. People giving because they're asked, on the other hand, highlights how well you manage the actual ask.

## People Give to Other People

The first thing to remember is that people are motivated to give to help other people, not to build buildings or fund agency expenses. People are motivated to give based on mission and mission impact. When fundraising, always put mission first. Fundraising is not about organizational needs; it is about other people and their needs.

Personal connection matters. The stronger the relationship between you and a potential partner, the more your feedback will mean to that partner. That's why I spend time talking about communication and relationship-building skills in a book meant to help increase your fundraising. To me, those skills are the crux of all your fundraising efforts. The more you hone and practice your communication and relationship-building skills, the more successful a fundraiser you will be.

Some people will give to you because they like you and want to help you succeed or make you happy. Your personal welfare is important to them. These people give solely to your cause because of the relationship they have with you.

> I once had a major funder whose brother was a client at the agency I worked for. During my tenure, she became dissatisfied with the services her brother was receiving and decided to look for another agency to provide her brother's supports. Because of the strength of the personal relationship I had built with her, she called me and told me that although she was dissatisfied with the services we provided, she was very satisfied with what I had done for her. She told me that although she was immediately leaving the agency, she would still make her regular contribution that year solely because of her relationship with me.
>
> **stories from the real world**

People giving based on relationship is why asking key volunteers to ask their friends to give works so well. Connection matters and people want to please their friends. The donors feel their donation contributes to something bigger than themselves, in this case, the relationship that exists between them and the asker.

A personal relationship may spur a gift each time an ask is made. In the United States, we are pretty good at asking for donations. But the key to long-term fundraising success is converting your one-time donors into repeat donors. And, we are notoriously bad at that. According to the Urban Institute's 2011 Fundraising Effectiveness Project, only 27 percent of all new organizational donors make a repeat gift.

So you need more than just a personal relationship if you are to succeed at garnering the resources you need for your organization to carry out its mission. You need to meet the personal needs of each individual. And to do that, you need to listen to your donors to find out what their needs are. You don't know unless they tell you.

The fundraising partnership, then, does not begin with your organization needing money. It begins with finding out the myriad of needs individuals have and meeting those needs in ways that are important and meaningful to them. Successful fundraising is not about your organization's needs. Successful fundraising is all about your donors and their needs.

And the basic human need that all individuals have in relationships is the need to be acknowledged and validated. If you acknowledge your partners and then validate their contributions, you will be successful beyond your wildest dreams.

First and foremost, acknowledge your donors' contributions. Thank them immediately. Get a written acknowledgement sent no later than twenty-four hours after a contribution. Thank them often. Thank them in ways that they best hear you. Send them the thank-you letter and put a personal note on it. Call them. Email them. Mention their gift in a newsletter. Mention their gifts at events. Name something after them. Thank them in ways they will find meaningful. Thank, thank, thank. Acknowledge donors and volunteers and their contributions often.

Validate your donors and volunteers. But don't just stop at thanking them for making a contribution. Let them know how their contribution made a

> **observation**
> In my twenty years of experience, not one donor or volunteer has ever been offended by being thanked too much.

difference in impacting the cause they care about.

Notice that I am not saying how the contribution made a difference to your organization. Although contributors may care deeply about your agency, ultimately, it is the impact that your agency makes that is important. Contributors care most about your ability to meet your mission and the impact your organization has on other people. Your organization's existence is just a means to an end.

So, when you validate your partners' contributions, talk about the end result, the impact they made toward the cause they care deeply about. In other words, make sure your communications about impact deal with mission-related impact rather than organizational survival or revenue issues.

### *People Give Because They're Asked*

People give because they're asked. In other words, you don't get if you don't ask. The ask is critical to your bringing in the revenue your organization needs.

There are many ways to ask for money from individuals. You can ask them to sponsor you in a walk- or dance-a-thon or other similar event. You can invite them to purchase tickets to your event. You can mail a letter to them. You can send out fundraising newsletters. You can email them. You can call them. You can meet with them face-to-face. The method that you choose to make the ask will depend on your donors' communication preferences. Generally, the higher the ask amount, the stronger the partnership, the more investment of resources, and the more personal the method of communication.

Know your donors. Know how they best receive what you have to say.

There are many books on the market that deal with asking and prospect research. I suggest starting with *Asking: A 59-Minute Guide to Everything Board Members, Volunteers, and Staff Must Know to Secure the Gift* by

Jerold Panas and *Asking About Asking: Mastering the Art of Conversational Fundraising* by M. Kent Stroman.

## Foundations

About 15 percent of all charitable giving in the United States is through foundations. Again, the exact percentages vary from year to year, but 15 percent is a good rough number.

Foundations want to give out money. Foundations exist to provide resources to organizations meeting specific needs. However, they recognize that there are many organizations out there that exist to meet the causes the foundation cares about. A foundation board's job is to find out what organization is best equipped to impact the identified issue.

> **practical tip**
>
> The variety of donor needs, the way donors best hear you, and the way they want to be asked is why your organization has a varied revenue mix. Make sure the fundraising methods you pick are based on the needs of your donors, not what's easiest for you to implement. And again, make sure the communication channels you choose to reach those donors are based on their preferences, not on what's easiest for you to do.

The first key to partnering with a foundation is to match missions. As partners, you will be two organizations with similar goals. In your search for foundation funding, it is imperative that you do your research and find out what needs a foundation devotes its resources to meeting and what kind of organization they are interested in supporting.

Foundations make available all kinds of information where you can find out about them. For starters, foundations must file a 990-PF, or tax return, every year with the IRS. These 990s are public information. They are readily available through the Foundation Center, GuideStar, and other repositories. Foundations usually publish application guidelines that are readily available by contacting the foundation. Many have websites and annual reports. Some publish research or position papers. For the most part, foundations find it in their best interest to make information about themselves readily available.

Foundations want to hear from organizations that make a relatively large impact on the issues they care about. However, foundations have limited resources. They cannot fund everyone. To get funded by a foundation today, your proposal needs to stand out from the rest, and the foundation board members need to connect with you.

So how do you stand out from the rest of the pack? First and foremost, you follow the funders' guidelines. It always surprises me how many organizations submit proposals that do not fit the stated guidelines.

It is in your best interest to only apply to foundations when you know you meet their funding guidelines. If you send a foundation an application that does not meet its guidelines, this tells the prospective funder that you either don't care enough to read the guidelines or follow them. Approaching a foundation without knowing about that foundation's interests shows disrespect. It says that you don't care enough about the foundation's needs; that only your need for money is important. That's not how you want to approach a potential partner.

> **practical tip**
> Shot-gunning, or sending the same request to many funders, never works. Always tailor your proposal to the needs of the funder.

Let the foundation know you are an expert in your field: know your issue and how it fits into the bigger picture. Give the foundation a vivid picture of the enormity of the community need you are addressing. *Community* needs, not organizational needs. (Remember, fundraising starts with identifying community needs, not yours.) With foundations, they tell you what their needs are and what issue they are interested in addressing. That issue should be the focus of your proposal. Not an organizational need. Remember, the need is never lack of a program or lack of resources. True need is always about what's going on in your community.

Let the foundation know how your organization fits into the broader scheme of things. Know your organizational strengths and weaknesses. Show how you play off your strengths and compensate for your weaknesses. Know about other organizations doing the same or similar things you do and know how you are different from these other organizations, what makes you uniquely qualified to address the issue at hand. Know where you collaborate with others and where you compete, and why.

Present yourself and your organization as professional and well-managed. Show that your organization uses resources wisely. Let the funder know why you do the things the way you do them. Show how your activities in this proposal are part of a bigger plan. Spell out how your request is part of something bigger than just the activities for which you are requesting funding.

Pay attention to the details. Have someone proofread your proposal for typos and spelling errors. Make sure your budget adds up correctly. Make sure the numbers in your narrative are the same as in the budget. Look professional, with consistent formatting and plenty of white space.

> Once, when I was at a funding panel and heard foundation officers talk, the stories they told of the proposals they receive shocked me. One foundation representative said her foundation consistently gets proposals with the name of the foundation spelled incorrectly. Another said his foundation regularly gets proposals addressed to the *wrong* foundation. Some mentioned that they often receive proposals with erasures or Wite Out; some even said they've received handwritten proposals! Often budget numbers are inconsistent or the budget doesn't add up correctly.
>
> Needless to say, when proposals are presented with these types of errors, the organization is automatically not seen in the best possible light.
>
> **stories from the real world**

Let foundations know you are trustworthy. Be honest in everything you say. Don't overpromise on your objectives. Don't underestimate or overestimate your organizational expenses or pad your budget. Be realistic with your timelines.

People who sit on foundation boards are usually well-informed professionals. They know what's going on out there in the field. They know how to gauge what is reasonable and what isn't. They might not have been introduced to your organization yet, but they know of many other organizations like yours.

And they are people too. They want to be treated with dignity and respect. They do not look kindly on people or organizations that try to fool them, tell them half-truths, or exaggerate the impact the organization is making. Always be truthful. Show funders you are a trustworthy partner.

Branding is an important concept with foundations. The foundation world is a relatively small one. Once your organization starts being known among a few funders, you will be talked about. You will be a known entity with a reputation. Believe me. I know from my experiences with foundation review panels. Once you have a certain reputation among funders, it takes a long time for those perceptions to change. For the better or for the worse.

The point of the story is not that you can slide by on your reputation. The point of the story is to underline the importance of successful branding.

There are many books in the market about approaching foundations. My recommendations are *"Thank You for Submitting Your Proposal:" A Foundation Director Reveals What Happens Next* by Martin Teitel, and my book *Confessions of a Successful Grants Writer: A Complete Guide for Discovering and Obtaining Funding*.

> At one job I held, I facilitated an allocation review committee. We would get far more requests for funding than we could possibly meet. I remember during one review session, a relatively poorly written proposal came in. I, being new to the community, didn't want to fund the request. To me, if the organization couldn't present itself in a professional manner, then what did that say about the organization's ability to do anything else in a professional manner?
>
> But the organization had a good brand. It was known for not being able to put together professional communications, but it was also known for delivering outstanding services and reaching a high-risk population in a high-need community in a way that few others did.
>
> The organization turned out to be one of the few that we funded that quarter.

**stories from the real world**

## Corporations

About 5 percent of all charitable giving in the United States is through corporations. As with the previous giving percentages, the exact percentage will vary from year to year, but generally remains right around 5 percent.

The first thing to remember about corporations is that they exist to *make* money. They are not in the business of giving away money. They might do it because it helps them make even more money or because they truly care about the community in which they are located. But always remember that businesses, first and foremost, are driven by profit.

I talked a little about partnering with for-profit organizations in **Chapter One** when I talked about identifying vendors as potential partners and again when I talked about identifying organizations with similar markets. Here, I will talk about how to present your organization as a good corporate partner.

To catch the attention of a for-profit business, you need to position your organization to look business-like. You can't look like a do-good service agency that doesn't care about money. For businesses to partner with you, you need to show them that your organization is financially viable and business savvy. A businessperson thinks in terms of satisfying market demand, financial returns, and strategic investments. As a potential partner, you need to understand and speak the businessperson's language. As with any partner, you need to start first with meeting the partner's needs. Begin by presenting your organization in ways that make sense to the businessperson.

### *Financial Performance*

You *must*, first and foremost, understand your organization's financial performance. For-profit companies exist for positive financial performance and know their numbers inside and out. For them to understand what your organization is trying to do, you must speak this language. It's what corporations understand. More importantly, it's how they measure success.

So if you need to, learn. Know your organization's asset, liability, and equity values. Understand your agency's cash-flow position. Be able to talk about revenues and expenses, as well as gross and net income. Figure out your programs' unit costs. Know your profit margin. Be able to cite your organization's return on investment.

> A good place to start understanding your agency's basic financial performance is with the organizational audit. When I first started developing corporate marketing materials, that's where I started. I asked our financial officer to go over the audit in detail with me so I understood all of the information it contained and would be prepared for the questions my potential partners could ask.
>
> I then took information from several years' worth of audits and summarized it in chart form. In that way, I was able to show my potential partners the relationship between my agency's assets, liabilities, and equity over time. The financial picture I presented backed up my story of agency growth, our increase in services and organizational capacity, and how many more people we were helping. I was able to show mission impact and organizational success in ways that my corporate partners could appreciate.
>
> **stories from the real world**

If your head is spinning right now, don't worry. I will talk more in depth about financial performance in **Chapters Six** and **Seven**. There are also many resources geared to understanding finances for nonfinancial managers. One of my favorites is *Streetsmart Financial Basics for Nonprofit Managers* by Thomas McLaughlin.

## *Market Performance*

In addition to financial performance, to catch a corporation's attention, you must also be able to speak about your organization in marketing terms. I've talked about knowing and sharing your markets in **Chapter One**. I have regularly mentioned branding and its importance to fundraising effectively. Now I'll talk about market positioning.

Market share and market positioning are key concepts in the corporate world. In the business world, significant market share can be a measure of sustainability. Assuming profitability, the more market share you have, the greater your percentage of sales in comparison to your competitors, the more sustainable your existence. Generally speaking, a greater market share is highly sought after.

How does this translate into the nonprofit world? We usually don't see ourselves or describe ourselves in these terms.

Well, the service we provide is our product. Our market is the number of people who experience the need we are meeting. Our percentage of market share is the number of people whose needs we are meeting divided by the total number of people whose need is being met by us and organizations like us. Our unmet market demand is the number of people whose needs are not being met by us or any organization like us. That unmet demand tells our business partners what our potential for growth is.

Unmet demand, to potential corporate partners, is one measure of whether your organization is a good investment for them or not. It tells them how much potential for growth you have in your market. If they are looking to reach shared markets, it gives them a measure of how much return on investment they'll get by partnering with you and your organization as you grow. And a good return on investment means potentially greater profits. They will want to be invested in your success.

It is sometimes very difficult for nonprofits to think of themselves in business terms. But it is a necessity if you are to reach the business community in a major way. You must understand the driving motivations of businesses if you are to partner in any meaningful way. In a partnership, both must experience a win if the partnership is to be successful. Understand what a win is for them. Understand

> **Sample Market-Share Calculations**
>
> Estimated number of people who need services like ours = our total market = 100,000
>
> The number of people we serve = 2,000 per year
>
> The number of additional people organizations like us serve = 20,000 additional people served
>
> 2,000 people served by us / 100,000 total market = 0.02, or 2 percent, our market share
>
> 100,000 total market – (2,000 people served by us + 20,000 people served by similar organizations) / 100,000 total market = (100,000 – 22,000) / 100,000 = 78,000 / 100,000, or 0.78, or 78 percent unmet market demand
>
> **Example**

their needs. That's where successful partnerships, especially fundraising partnerships, start—with the needs and motivations of your partner.

## Government

A significant portion of revenues for many nonprofits, particularly those in human services, come from governmental sources. Working with governmental funders is a whole different experience than working with individuals, foundations, or corporations.

To understand how to approach and deal with governmental funders, you must understand that the process is ruled by legislation. The main goal here is to know and abide by the rules of the law. You cultivate personal relationships with legislators, the ones who make the laws. Before applying for funding, you must know the laws and regulations and format your proposal accordingly. After receiving funding, you make the program officer's life easier by abiding by the regulations contained in the legislation. To receive continued funding, you submit complete and timely reports with data required by the funding legislation. Rules, regulations, and reports will take over your life when you get into the world of governmental funding.

The best suggestion I can make if you are going after governmental funding is to know all the players, understand the legislative process, and keep current with all the legislation and associated regulations governing the funding you are pursuing.

Know the legislative and political process. You will need this information to advocate for certain bills as they move through the separate houses of state and federal government. Know who is in power and what powers they have. Know the committees your legislators serve on, where legislation first shows up, and where it is modified.

> **practical tip**
> 
> Know who the players are. Get to know your legislators. Help them help the community. Be an expert in your field for them. If they have helped you in any way or supported legislation that helps your organization or the people you serve, publicize it for them. Tell your constituents what is happening. Let the legislators know you can be their friend and support them.

Know how the committee structure changes as the political parties gain and lose power. All of this knowledge will help you know where to target your advocacy efforts for maximum effect.

It is especially important to be on top of the legislative process and players when federal and state budgets are being negotiated. A significant portion of federal spending passes down to states and then, in turn, passes down to more local units of government. If your organization relies on or is thinking of pursuing governmental funding, you need to be aware of the budget process to be able to predict future funding and cash flow. More than once, the federal or state budget has not been passed and the federal or state government has shut down. Which means payments are not made. Which affects when revenues are received. If your organization relies on governmental funding for a significant portion of its budget, there had better be a plan in place to juggle cash flow and keep operations going to serve the people you serve in case your funding stops flowing.

Sometimes, too, programs are cut or de-funded. If your organization has governmental funding and your program is cut or de-funded, you have lots of problems to deal with. Your organization's revenues will decrease, which affects organizational financial performance and the ability to obtain credit. Management might have to cut hours or lay off staff, which affects employee morale as well as organizational capacity. Worst of all, you might have to turn away clients or discontinue services altogether.

> In good economic times when tax revenues are stable, governmental funding can seem like a godsend. The funding is adequate and continues for long periods of time. A nonprofit's dream.
>
> Many times, organizations in that position become lax and begin to over-rely on the governmental revenue streams. They begin to think they don't need to cultivate other types of donors and thus neglect formulating and implementing a comprehensive development plan.
>
> I know of several nonprofits that were caught short like this in the current economic downturn. Now, they barely have enough revenue to function, much less grow, their development efforts.
>
> **watch out!**

The above scenarios illustrate why it is important to keep up with legislative and political processes. If you are a small development shop and you receive or are going to pursue governmental funding, make sure the advocacy part of your job is covered. If you are a large enough organization that you have someone else on staff who takes care of government relations, then make you sure you work with this person and augment these efforts.

The last point I want to make is to research and be familiar with *all* the legislation pertaining to the funding you are pursuing. Many times, current legislation is based on previous legislation. And that legislation, in turn, might be based on even older legislation. All those regulations will apply to your funding request. For me, researching all those laws and regulations is tedious, boring work. But it is necessary so that you don't get your organization into a situation where it cannot deliver on its promises and has to give back funding. Or does not follow all the rules and ends up in litigation. Or ends up with a project costing more than the revenues received. Know the legislation and all the regulations pertaining to it. The hours of research are well worth the effort.

---

I once wrote and received a $600,000 governmental housing grant. We were overjoyed.

That is, until we learned that the legislation required higher construction wages than we were prepared to absorb. This requirement was not readily evident in the 2009 and 1974 legislation I had researched. The 2009 legislation was governed by legislation passed in 1974 which, in turn, was governed by legislation passed in the 1940s. The determination of higher construction wages was in the 1940s legislation. I had not gone back far enough.

The requirement for higher construction wages made the project unfeasible as planned. The organization had to scrap the investment in the engineering plans and architectural drawings it had paid for and go back to the drawing board. We also used up a lot of political capital in going back to the politicians with a project that had changed in the scope of what was originally promised.

**stories from the real world**

Know the rules you're going to play by before you get into the game. Know how the rules are made, who makes the rules, and who changes the rules. Know how long the game will last. Know what will move you forward toward a win and what will get you disqualified. Know what happens when the players change. Know how to get out of the game if you don't want to play anymore. Know what can stop the game and what happens if it stops. Be prepared for anything.

Different funding partners have different values, different motivations, and different perspectives. Know your partners and where they're coming from. Speak their language so they understand you and want to get to know your organization. Present your organization in their terms. Show them you have many of the same interests they do. Build a relationship with them starting with their needs, not yours. Acknowledge and validate them. You will go far if you do.

**To Recap**

- ◆ Develop relationships based on meeting donor needs.
- ◆ Acknowledge and validate your donors.
- ◆ Match missions and follow guidelines.
- ◆ Pay attention to your brand.
- ◆ Know your organization's financial and market performance indicators.
- ◆ Be aware of all the legislation and its political environment when pursuing governmental funding.

# Chapter Five

## The Larger Context

**IN THIS CHAPTER**

- The role of corporate culture
- Easing the effects of the economy
- Navigating the political system
- Working through the media

A partnership does not develop in a vacuum. The partners you choose to pursue and the benefits of those partnerships are influenced by the environments in which you both function. Context determines how you are perceived by your partners and whether they believe your organization is their best option. How you and your partners operationalize (that is, design implementation processes for) your partnership agreements is heavily determined by this same context. In this chapter I will explore the influence of the greater environment on potential partnerships. I also talk about common strategies used to influence the greater contextual environment, such as the effects of culture, economy, political systems, and the media, in our favor.

### Cultural Values and Beliefs

Our values are largely determined by the culture in which we grow up and choose to operate. Cultural values and beliefs are passed on to us through our societal institutions: our families, our educational system, our economic system, and our justice system. To survive and function in any society, we must abide by that society's norms, values, and beliefs. If we don't abide by the cultural norms, we are punished until we do. If we continue to violate the norms or our violations are egregious enough, we will then be removed from the society and not allowed to operate in it. These tenets hold true whether we are talking about large societal groups, like countries, or smaller ones, such as nonprofit organizations.

***Corporate Values***

Every organization has its own corporate culture, that is, its own set of written and unwritten rules for behavior. These codes for behavior are based on a company's values. Smart companies explicitly state their values in a values statement and communicate them to their constituencies so everyone knows what the organization stands for. And, in turn, the organization is transparent in its reporting, so people know the organization behaves in a way consistent with its stated values. This way, everybody involved with the organization—board members, employees, volunteers, vendors, donors, and collaborators—knows what principles will guide that organization's interactions.

Stating organizational values, communicating them, and showing how your organization lives up to them builds a strong brand. Building a strong brand with various constituencies leads to a lot of desirable outcomes:

- ◆ good business relationships
- ◆ ability to attract good employees
- ◆ improved employee morale
- ◆ better workplace operations
- ◆ increased employee retention
- ◆ ability to attract new clients
- ◆ improved client satisfaction
- ◆ increased client loyalty

- ability to attract good volunteers and board members
- ability to attract donors
- improved donor loyalty

An organization with a strong, positive brand will not only function better, it will realize a greater market share. Greater market share can mean greater financial stability and potential for growth. And when growth is managed correctly, it means better financial performance. Which means more resources for you to be better able to meet your agency's mission. This, in turn, means a stronger brand. And so on.

Know the values inherent in your organization's culture.

### Culture Clashes

Sometimes cultures clash and the going is rough. Just because cultures clash and there is dissonance, doesn't mean the partnership is a bad idea or won't work. It just means you have a lot of work to do; you each have to hear what the other has to say to find out if the partnership will work or not. For example, a large corporate nonprofit, such as a health-care center, will probably have a very different culture than a small community arts organization. They might have a hard time working together if the cultures clash too much. But they might be perfect partners in providing art therapy or psychodrama programs to patients.

Cultures consist of many elements. Take language, for instance. Differences in language are easy to see when you both speak totally different languages, such as French and English. But those differences are harder to see when you both speak English, especially if both you and your partner

> **practical tip**
> 
> A positive cycle—from positive branding leading to greater market share leading to greater financial stability leading to better financial performance leading to more mission fulfillment leading to better branding and so on—can be built no matter how big or how small your agency is, what the economy is, or how the political winds blow. If your agency is meeting relevant needs, knows who it is and what it stands for, and can back its claims up, it will be a leader in its field no matter what the environment.

> **stories from the real world**
>
> I have worked with a multitude of organizations throughout my career and each had their own definition of what a major gift was. In one, a major gift meant a donation from an individual that was over $500. In another, a major gift meant a donation of $10,000 or more from any type of contributor: individual, foundation, or corporation. In one, they considered planned giving as part of their major gift program. In another, planned giving was reported separately.

are from similar organizations or backgrounds. The fact is corporate cultures differ from one organization to the next. What is said in one organization might mean something totally different in another.

In any partnership you choose to undertake, I cannot overemphasize the importance of the feedback loop. The feedback loop is critical to understanding exactly what your potential partner can offer, how your partner can deliver on that offer, and what that partner expects in return. I talked about the feedback loop in **Chapter Two**.

Another cultural element to consider is one of method. Why an organization does what it does and how it does it is based on many factors—history, leadership, and life cycle, to name a few. No one organization does things in the exact same way as another organization.

Sometimes when people see the vast differences in how their respective organizations are operationalized, they think that the difference in operational processes necessarily negates a successful partnership. Not true. There are a thousand ways to skin a cat. Choosing different methods does not mean there is no agreement. It only means partners have their own methods.

Why we do what we do in the way we do it is a values decision. Whether we make that decision deliberately or as part of our culture, our actions reflect the values we live by.

Organizational operations, then, are expressions of organizational values. If you are looking at a partnership in which you and your potential partner's methods are at odds, dig deeper to identify the values behind those methods. You might connect on values, even if you don't on method.

> I once met with a business association that was interested in attracting good employees. My organization was interested in housing for people with disabilities. The business association believed in self-regulation and hated government interference of any kind. My organization relied heavily on government funding. Very different cultures, very different missions, and very different ways of achieving outcomes.
>
> But one value that we both held was safety. We connected on the goal of safe neighborhoods: the business association wanted safe neighborhoods for its employees to live in, and we wanted the same thing for our clients. But because we knew we both valued safety, we were also able to promote our mission of integrating people with disabilities into the community through that value. We met the association's need for safety because we could openly address their concerns about dealing with people with disabilities. Reciprocally, we could address our concerns about how people with disabilities are often taken advantage of. We were able to begin a strong partnership around a common value despite our enormous differences.
>
> *stories from the real world*

Just because you connect with another partner, however, doesn't mean the partnership is worth pursuing. You will first have to do a cost-benefit analysis to see if you are actually coming out with a win. I talk more about financial considerations in **Chapters Six** and **Seven**.

## The Economy

According to the National Center for Charitable Statistics, in 2011, nonprofits contributed goods and services worth $751 billion to the U.S. gross domestic product (GDP), 5.5 percent of GDP. The number of nonprofits has increased 25 percent in the last ten years: from 1.26 million in 2001 to 1.57 million in 2011. The growth rate of the nonprofit sector has surpassed the growth rates of both the business and government sectors. According to Bureau of Labor Statistics data, nonprofits now employ 10.5 million workers, or nearly 10 percent of all private workers in the United States, making the nonprofit workforce the third-largest in the United States, trailing only manufacturing and retail but far ahead of construction, transportation, and finance. The nonprofit sector is a huge part of, and is greatly affected by, the nation's economy.

## *The Effects of the Economy*

In a good economy, things go relatively well for the nonprofit: Overall revenues stay steady or increase, revenues keep pace with costs, and demand for services stays steady. As the economy expands, so does the nonprofit sector. Times are relatively good.

But in a bad economy, things are very strained for the nonprofit. A nonprofit is going to be squeezed just like everyone else in a down economy. Donation revenues decrease as unemployment climbs and donations from individuals decline. Government revenues decrease as employment, income, and sales tax revenues decline due to higher unemployment and under-employment. Corporate contributions decline as people rein in spending and company profits tumble. And foundation contributions decrease as stock market values and interest rates fall, causing foundation endowment values to be worth less with a smaller investment return. In a bad economy, there is just not as much money to go around. You need to keep a close watch on local and national economic fluctuations on a regular basis.

In addition to reduced overall resources, the number of people demanding services increases. More people have more needs. Not only has the pie gotten smaller, but the number of people who need to be fed has gotten larger. In a slow economy, there is an increased number of nonprofits competing for a smaller pot of available money, with more demand for services than they can handle.

And the result is not a pretty picture. With reduced revenues, organizations need to cut costs. With wages and benefits usually being the largest expense in the budget, that's where the ax tends to fall: reduced benefits, frozen or reduced wages, reduced hours, and layoffs are the result. Employee morale plummets.

At the same time, the organization is faced with increased demand for services, more unmet need than it can handle. Program costs might increase. What ends up happening is that people don't get served and need is not met. Current organizational resources, including staff, are strained to the limit. Staff members might feel as though they are running in place and can never catch up or get ahead. Employee morale plummets even further.

Adequate staffing and good employee morale are important to organizational partnerships because the employees are the ones who make the mission happen. They are the organization's mission in action. They are the ones delivering your organization's services and satisfying the clients. Your organization's staff is integral to your brand. Staff performance tells your partners whether your organization can live up to its promises or not. In many ways, your organization's greatest resource is its staff.

### *Combating the Economy*

So how can you combat some of the effects of a down economy? Partnerships. You can increase revenues, decrease costs, and increase organizational capacity through partnerships with donors, volunteers, employees, and vendors. You can also collaborate with agencies with similar goals and organizations with similar markets. I talked about identifying partners in **Chapter One** and reaching those partners in **Chapter Four**.

Organizations that have strong partnerships with all of their constituencies have an easier time weathering the storms of a bad economy than those that don't. An organization with many strong partnerships has many more resources on which to rely when times get tough than an agency with fewer or weaker partnerships. This is true no matter what size the agency.

In bad economic times, foundations and governmental funders tend to increase the call for collaborations among nonprofits. The idea is to reduce the administrative expenses related to operating a number of nonprofits doing the same thing. If you want

> I work for an agency today that is in the situation many small nonprofits find themselves in: it is struggling to manage the greater demand for services coupled with the decrease in resources to meet these demands. When I came on board, the agency was in crisis. But the agency had built tremendous partnerships with its staff, volunteers, donors, and community. No one gave up on this agency. All the partners stuck with it and did whatever they could to ensure that the agency remained viable. The agency was able to tap into a multitude of resources to ride out the financial crisis.
>
> **stories from the real world**

to be one of the nonprofits to be considered for funding from these sources, you better show how your organization collaborates with a number of partners.

When we hear about collaborative cost reductions, most of us think automatically of collaborating with organizations providing similar services to similar consumers. And there might be some synergy with a similar organization. But chances are that since there is more than enough need in the nonprofit world, both organizations must exist in order to meet the demand for services. Many people think of mergers, but that option is extreme, as it means the organizations in question cease to be partners as they meld into one organization. Such "partnerships" are beyond the scope of this book.

Showing strong collaborations does not necessarily mean partnering with similar organizations or merging in some way. For example, two very different nonprofits can share space. Or many nonprofits can join together as a group to purchase health-care benefits. Or a nonprofit can receive in-kind services from a for-profit for business planning or marketing support. Or a nonprofit might increase its productivity through the use of unpaid staff. All of these partnerships allow an agency to reduce its expenses or increase its organizational capacity. All of these types of partnerships should be highlighted in your organization's requests for funding, especially from foundations and government agencies.

> **practical tip**
> In application after application, funders constantly ask me about the type of collaborations my organization has in place. The more partnerships I can document, the better off I am.

In bad economic times, your vendors might be your best partners. They, too, will be struggling, as people have less discretionary income and the company's consumer base shrinks. Your repeat business will be important to the company. If you have a large staff or a large volunteer base, the additional market exposure might be of interest to them. You might also be an attractive partner to them as a cause to support as they define themselves as giving back to the community. They might be looking for relatively low-cost marketing avenues; your nonprofit might fit that bill exactly.

Bad economic times lead to turbulent political times. Politicians may be even more willing than usual to partner with you, especially if you have a good brand. Politicians want to be associated with success. They want to have a part in your success so they can tell voters how they have helped the community. You might even be able to give them an audience of potential voters, through a special event or a client or volunteer forum.

## The Political System

As I stated in **Chapter Four**, if your organization relies on or is thinking of pursuing governmental funding, it is imperative that you know how government works. You need to know how legislation is made, how it is funded, how it is interpreted, and how it is enforced. Even if you don't receive governmental funding, it is still a good idea to keep tabs on legislative initiatives, since they might directly affect your clients and the services they need. Legislation might also affect those organizations you partner with and determine what your partner might or might not be able to do.

### *Advocating for Your Cause*

Legislation is passed or not passed by legislators, who are elected by voters. To influence voters, political candidates actively

> **stories from the real world**
>
> One human-services agency I worked for had this formula down pat. It held voter registration drives among its client base. It held candidate forums for its clients. It also had five hundred people show up to its gala to which it invited the local politicians. Each politician who showed up got two minutes of fame on the podium. We were happy, the politicians were happy, and our advocacy agenda always seemed to get the attention of the politicians.

> **practical tip**
>
> A college course in political science helped me understand how the different branches of government work. Such courses are readily available through community continuing education courses or local two-year and four-year colleges. If you want to understand more about how government works, I highly recommend that you pursue these and other avenues for enhancing your professional education.

market themselves to their constituents. How much market exposure candidates get is mostly determined by how much money the candidates are able to amass to pay for their marketing activities. And money flows from individuals, corporations, the government, and political action committees. It is important, then, to directly influence not only individual legislators but also the larger context in which they operate.

The expanse of influence you need is why partnering with as many others as you can in advocacy campaigns is important. Industry and professional organizations often offer national and state advocacy as part of their product array to member organizations. These associations are very adept at orchestrating advocacy campaigns. Industry advocacy organizations specialize in impacting the players at different stages of the legislative process and are well worth your organizational investment in them.

Board members, employees, donors, volunteers—all are people you can ask to join you in specific advocacy campaigns. Legislation that affects them and their well-being will be of interest to them, and they should be offered the opportunity to influence it. These constituents are all heavily invested in your mission as well, and they will care about your organization's well-being.

As will your other partners—your vendors, for instance. If legislation will affect the ability of your organization to do business with them and you are a good customer, they're going to care about your well-being. In addition, look at your corporate partners. They see their contributions to you as an investment. They will be looking for a favorable return on that investment. If certain legislation will affect that return, they might be interested in supporting your agenda.

> When I was working for one agency whose mission included safe and affordable housing, I sent out a link to comment on the HUD strategic plan that was being finalized and asked all my partners to comment on it as they saw fit. I also told them which parts of that plan were relevant to our organization's functioning and how those parts could impact the supports our clients received. I was surprised not only by how many participated, but also who participated. I did not expect the response I got from my donors and my vendors.
>
> **stories from the real world**

*Building Relationships with Legislators*

To stay in power, legislators need to satisfy those backing them—individuals, corporations, and political action committees—that they have met their constituency's needs. In order to affect a legislator's vote on an issue, your organization needs to inform the legislators about the needs of their constituencies. Likewise, when legislators deliver a win, your organization should also promote those legislators among their constituencies.

There are many ways to inform a legislator about your constituents' needs. You can prepare a packet of information for them, highlighting the severity of the community need you meet and any evidence of how well you meet it. You can arrange for a visit to their office or a tour of yours. You can invite them to an event. You can testify at a public hearing. You can attend an event that you know they are attending and network with them. You can get to know their legislative staff and be a resource for them. You can have your constituents write letters, make phone calls, or email them. The possibilities are endless.

But it is not only about getting the legislator to know you and your cause. It is also about delivering a win for them. It is a true partnership.

This is another reason why you want to know your legislators and the legislative process. You want to know who your political supporters are and who your detractors are. And you want to reward your supporters.

The way you reward politicians is by enhancing their market exposure. Do you invite politicians to speak in front of voters? Do you acknowledge them at your public events? If you have a large staff or volunteer base, do you have forums where politicians can come and say a few words? Do you thank them for their votes when it goes your way? Do you inform your constituents of the politicians' votes on legislation important to you? In organizational marketing materials, when you publish pictures of events, do you include those of the politicians who came and supported you? Do you recognize public leaders as award recipients? All of these avenues are ways to deliver positive market exposure, a win, for a politician.

## Regulatory Bodies

Regulatory bodies also influence the partners you pursue and the partnership agreements that ensue from those relationships.

> **watch out!**
> If you receive governmental funding, make sure your communications with legislators fall within the category of "informing the public," not "endorsing a candidate." Strict IRS rules (see IRS publication 557) specify how governmental funding can be spent. A nonprofit can lose its tax-exempt status if it violates those rules. Know where those lines are.

If you are government funded, you are probably government regulated to some extent. You might have regulations that dictate who you can serve, what services you can deliver, how you deliver services, or how long you can serve someone. This funding partnership directly affects how you operationalize your mission and what impact you can make. Sometimes governmental funders also dictate what type of other partnerships you can and can't pursue. This is why nongovernmental funding is so important—usually the restrictions are not so limiting.

On the other hand, if you need a governmental license or accreditation to function, you can use that requirement to better position yourself in the funding market. It is a strong statement to say that a governmental entity has found you worthy of their funding for however many years. It gives your organization automatic credibility. For example, saying that the Department of Education selected your program for a $100,000 award, which it has doubled in the past five years, gives validity to your organization and its accomplishments. Stating that you have a partnership with the Department of Health that spans twenty years speaks to the ongoing need for your services and your ability to fulfill partnership obligations.

Sometimes organizations seek voluntary accreditations, such as CARF (formerly known as the Crediting Agency for Rehabilitation Facilities) or the American Association of Suicidology or other industry accrediting bodies, to better position themselves in their various markets. There are many accreditation organizations out there. Voluntary accreditation agencies have standards an organization must meet, but usually without many of the same restrictions as governmental accreditation agencies. Sometimes these partnerships cost money that your organization might or might not feel is worth the investment, depending on financial and market returns. I talk about financial considerations in **Chapters Six** and **Seven**.

Some organizations pay for staff to belong to professional organizations and become certified or accredited in their field. The benefits of doing so might outweigh the costs. If your organization employs staff who have advanced educational degrees, professional certifications, or professional licenses (such as Registered Nurse, Licensed Clinical Social Worker, Certified Public Accountant, Certified Fund Raising Executive, Grants Professional Certified), use that to your advantage. Often, staff credentials are overlooked in anything beyond the recruiting process. Take advantage of the partnerships that your staff members maintain.

## The Media

The media is a powerful societal influence. The media informs the public and shapes perceptions. Most nonprofits crave positive media attention. Mastering public relations is an endeavor well worth investing in.

Press coverage is important because it informs a large public about your cause and your organization. Corporate partners love it when they are mentioned because it associates them with caring about their community. In short, positive press coverage communicates an organization's brand to a wide audience that consists of many of your organization's constituencies. It is a cost-effective marketing tool.

> Showing your staff's credibility through neutral, third-party credentials given by outside professional organizations speaks to the quality of employees your organization attracts and the services your organization is able to provide, which is vitally important to your brand.
>
> 👍 **practical tip**

Most nonprofits think of improved media relations as generating better press releases. Media relations, though, goes far beyond just the press release. Media relations is about paid advertising and consistent exposure. It is about writing letters to the editor in response to issues that are important to your organization. It is about keeping your media contacts informed about your organization. It is about being a resource for the reporters in your area of expertise. It is about staying abreast of current events. It is about messaging (crafting and sending messages) and consistency in messaging.

Like all your relationships, a relationship with the media starts with them and their needs, rather than with you and yours. Know their processes and deadlines. Know their priorities. Know their preferences. Know what's important to them. When you're dealing with the press, be aware that there are many more competitors for the media's attention than just your nonprofit or even the world of nonprofits. Getting them to notice you and care about your needs means getting to know them and caring about their needs first.

Make sure your material is interesting to the public, not just to your organization. No one outside your organization cares about your innovative operations, your events, the honors you receive, or the money you raised. What the readers care about is how your organization affects their lives. How are you making the world a better place? What is your contribution to society? How are you making the community better? What have you done that will help people live better lives?

For example, few people care if my organization has a gala and who the sponsors are. They might care, though, that community businesses are helping people find assistance and hope through the only crisis line in the community. Few people care that one of my organization's clients spoke at a conference. But they might care if I tell them how that client overcame childhood trauma to beat the odds, became successful, and is now helping professionals help others like him. Few people care what legislation my organization supports. But they might care if my organization helped pass legislation that will help their neighborhoods be safer. Make sure your stories are relevant to the public.

Like all partnerships, developing relationships with the media takes an investment on your organization's part. Dealing with the media is usually a cost that generates little, if any, revenue. How you support cost centers like this is part of your organization's overall financial strategy. I talk more about financial considerations in **Chapters Six** and **Seven**.

Culture, the economy, politics, regulatory bodies, and the media are all part of the bigger context in which your organization operates. They heavily influence how your organization operates and the partners with whom you choose to develop relationships. Environmental influence is not solely a one-way relationship, however, as you work to ease the negative effects of your environment and positively influence those who control that environment.

> I am a good writer, but I have found that writing for the media is very different than writing grants, fundraising materials, or books. Many times, I am so close to my organization and so excited about its accomplishments that I think everyone will want to know about them and find them as exciting as I do. Sometimes I have difficulty determining the perspective that makes a story newsworthy; that is, if my story is "dog bites human" or "human bites dog" to them.
>
> Therefore, I have found it extremely cost-beneficial to invest in professional help. My time is used more effectively and I get more press coverage. I hire a press consultant to work with me. I could have also invested in some volunteer recruitment and training for an unpaid staff member to help me or I could have asked a corporation for in-kind professional services.
>
> *stories from the real world*

## To Recap

- ◆ Identify and communicate the values that drive your organization's corporate culture.

- ◆ Rely on all your partners and the resources they bring to the table, especially in tough economic times.

- ◆ Know the political system and legislative process. Ask *all* your partners to help influence it.

- ◆ Help legislators get the positive market exposure they need.

- ◆ Use organizational and staff credentials to better position your agency in the market.

- ◆ Go beyond the press release to optimize partnerships with the media.

# Chapter Six

## Financial Considerations

### IN THIS CHAPTER

- Determining total costs: direct, indirect, and opportunity costs
- Net income
- Pricing strategies

You should know what costs your organization will incur and how those costs affect the bottom line before you embark on any partnership. In fundraising, how much money you bring in is *not* the name of the game. What is important is how much money you have left over after taking into account the costs related to raising those funds. It doesn't matter how much gross revenue you raise if you don't cover your costs. Without enough net income, your organization will not survive.

In the following pages, I briefly cover the concepts of utilizing a chart of accounts, budgeting, calculating costs, weighing opportunity costs, and measuring profitability. For a more complete discussion about how to use these financial tools, see my workbook *Succeed in Your Nonprofit Funding Partnerships: Analyzing Their Costs and Benefits*.

### Determining Total Costs

Many nonprofits often don't calculate total costs when considering fundraising partnerships and thus don't know how much money to ask for. They don't target their asks well and end up asking for too few dollars or operating in partnerships that aren't structured to achieve their full financial potential. The three types of costs that I consider in determining my organization's total costs are direct costs, indirect costs, and opportunity costs.

## *Direct Costs*

Direct costs are costs associated directly with a specific program or project. They are the easiest of all the costs to calculate.

Direct costs are not just the expenses related to staff and materials associated with the project; direct costs include a broad array of direct expenses. For example, if your organization runs a mentoring program for youth, your direct program costs might include the following:

- ◆ Outreach materials to attract youth
- ◆ Outreach and recruitment activities to attract mentors
- ◆ Training the mentors
- ◆ Computer equipment, software, and Internet fees
- ◆ Rent and utilities
- ◆ Telephone costs
- ◆ Office supplies
- ◆ Staff to carry out the program, including recruitment, salaries, and benefits
- ◆ Staff training activities, such as professional memberships, publications, and conferences
- ◆ Staff travel

Notice that I am including a lot of costs that are not normally thought of as direct program costs, such as rent, utilities, and classified advertising. You must remember to include *all* the direct costs, not just the obvious ones such as program staff and outreach materials. It is a good idea to include program and finance staff when you are planning your budget to ensure you include all the organizational costs involved in running the program.

You can also go to your organization's chart of accounts for a complete list of costs. A chart of accounts is a listing of all the accounts where your organization's total revenues, expenses, assets, liabilities, and equity are recorded. A chart of accounts can be obtained from your organization's accounting department or bookkeeper.

Fringe benefits are usually expressed as a percentage of salary. Sometimes, especially in governmental grants, fringe benefits need to be spelled out. For a breakdown of fringe benefits, you can go to your payroll administrator or accounting department. For the total percentage of salary, just add up the separate percentages.

An annual budget with the above direct costs might look like this:

## Sample Youth Program Direct Cost Budget #1

| Expenses | |
|---|---|
| *Personnel* | |
| Program Director | $ 40,000 |
| Training Coordinator | $ 30,000 |
| Volunteer Coordinator | $ 30,000 |
| | $ 100,000 |
| Fringe Benefits (@ 30%) | $ 30,000 |
| Total Personnel | $ 130,000 |
| *Nonpersonnel* | |
| Youth Outreach Materials | $ 1,000 |
| Mentor Outreach Materials | $ 1,000 |
| Training Workbooks | $ 250 |
| Computers (2 @ $500 ea.) | $ 1,000 |
| Printers (2 @ $200 ea.) | $ 400 |
| Software Licenses | $ 150 |
| Internet Fees ($30/mo. for 12 mos.) | $ 360 |
| Rent ($1,200/mo. for 12 mos.) | $ 14,400 |

| Expenses | |
|---|---|
| Utilities ($200/mo. for 12 mos.) | $ 2,400 |
| Phone ($50/mo. for 12 mos.) | $ 600 |
| Office Supplies | $ 500 |
| Classified Advertising | $ 200 |
| Dues and Subscriptions | $ 375 |
| Conference Fees | $ 1,200 |
| Local Travel | $ 250 |
| Long Distance Travel | $ 1,200 |
| Total Nonpersonnel | $ 25,285 |
| Total Personnel | $130,000 |
| Total Expenses | $ 155,285 |

When an organization operates more than one program, oftentimes a staff person might work part-time in one program and part-time in another. In a budget, staff time is expressed in terms of full-time equivalents, or FTEs. For example, if two staff people hold the same position and work full-time in the same program, the budget line for that position would be two FTEs. If, however, one staff person works half-time in one position, the budget line for that position would be .5 FTE. If one person works full-time and one person works half-time in the same program, you would have 1.5 FTEs.

Percentage of FTE is based on how many hours of a person's time is spent on a particular activity. These percentages can be formally calculated by periodically undergoing time studies, where an employee who works full-time covering more than one program documents time spent over a week or two in fifteen-minute increments. You would then add all the increments spent in one program and divide that by the total hours you are using as your base. That gives you a relatively good percentage FTE.

Make sure that when you get the results of your time studies, the staff FTE percentages line up with the requirements of your funding sources. If they don't match, adjust them. If you have added or deleted staff, you will want to renegotiate your personnel costs with your funder. If funding has increased or decreased, you will want to revise staff job descriptions and how much time staff members are spending on any one activity. You don't want to see more than one revenue source covering the same person doing the same job in the same program, particularly if you have government funding where getting paid twice for the same service is illegal.

A budget with various amounts of full-time equivalents might look like this:

> **Example**
>
> Employee A spends ten hours a week in Program A and thirty hours a week in Program B. To calculate Employee A's percentage FTE in each program, the formula would look like this:
>
> Program A: 10 / 40 = 0.25 FTE
>
> Program B: 30 / 40 = 0.75 FTE

### Sample Youth Program Direct Cost Budget #2

| Expenses | |
|---|---|
| *Personnel* | |
| Executive Director (.25 FTE @ $70,000/yr.) | $ 17,500 |
| Program Director (1 FTE @ $40,000/yr.) | $ 40,000 |
| Training Coordinator (1 FTE @ $30,000/yr.) | $ 30,000 |
| Volunteer Coordinators (2 FTE's @ $30,000/yr.) | $ 60,000 |
| | **$ 147,500** |
| Fringe Benefits (@ 30%) | $ 44,250 |
| **Total Personnel** | **$ 191,750** |
| *Nonpersonnel* | |
| Youth Outreach Materials | $ 1,500 |
| Mentor Outreach Materials | $ 1,500 |
| Training Workbooks | $ 500 |
| Computers (2 @ $500 ea.) | $ 1,000 |
| Printers (2 @ $200 ea.) | $ 400 |
| Software Licenses | $ 300 |

| Expenses | |
|---|---|
| Internet Fees ($30/mo. for 12 mos.) | $ 360 |
| Rent ($1,200/mo. for 12 mos.) | $ 14,400 |
| Utilities ($200/mo. for 12 mos.) | $ 2,400 |
| Phone ($50/mo. for 12 mos.) | $ 600 |
| Office Supplies | $ 1,000 |
| Classified Advertising | $ 500 |
| Dues and Subscriptions | $ 1,000 |
| Conferences | $ 1,200 |
| Local Travel | $ 250 |
| Long Distance Travel | $ 2,400 |
| Total Nonpersonnel | $ 29,310 |
| Total Personnel | **$ 191,750** |
| Total Expenses | **$ 221,060** |

Sometimes, an organization is so small that the total organization *is* the program, that is, the organization does only one thing. In such cases, all your costs will be direct costs and your program budget will be the same as your organizational budget. This is common for organizations that have only one service offering.

The above cost budgets are the types you would use when preparing proposals for foundation, governmental or, sometimes, corporate funding. Funders want to see how their dollars will be used and how much additional funding you have, that is, how leveraged their investment will be. They are also looking at a project's or program's feasibility, that is, whether costs are reasonable and customary and whether you will be able to generate enough revenue so that the project or program at least breaks even. You must have enough revenue to cover all your expenses or the project is not viable.

These types of budgets are also crucial for you to construct around special events and fundraising appeals. Often agencies only calculate the obvious direct expenses, such as venue, printing, mailing, and award expenses. In reality, you also have allocated staff time—fundraising, administrative, and management, as well as telephone costs and office supplies.

An event budget that outlines all your direct costs might look like this:

## Sample Gala Direct Cost Budget

| Expenses | |
|---|---:|
| Invitation Printing | $ 2,000 |
| Mailing | $ 2,000 |
| Ad Journal | $ 2,000 |
| Venue (including food and entertainment) | $ 15,000 |
| Honoree Awards | $ 500 |
| Flowers | $ 1,000 |
| Photographer | $ 750 |
| Fundraising Coordinator Salary (.33 FTE @ $45,000/yr.) | $ 15,000 |
| Fringe Benefits (.30 of salary) | $ 5,000 |
| Clerical Support (100 hours @ $15/hr.) | $ 1,500 |
| Telephone | $ 100 |
| Office Supplies (paper, printer cartridge, copying, etc.) | $ 150 |
| Total Direct Costs | $ 45,000 |

Your direct costs, however, do not tell the whole story. You need to also add in your indirect costs to get the complete picture.

### *Indirect Costs*

Indirect costs are commonly referred to as overhead costs. They are the costs not directly attributable to a specific program or project, such as marketing, accounting, and human-resource staff. In larger organizations, that list will also probably include executive management. In smaller organizations, the percentage FTE spent on these activities by the executive director is the overhead cost. (In proposal budgets, the overhead cost rate

> Overhead Costs / Total Budget = Overhead Cost Rate
>
> $30,000 Organizational Overhead Costs / $300,000 Total Organizational Budget = 0.10 Overhead Cost Rate

**Example**

is generally referred to as "general and administrative" or G&A.)

Indirect costs can be calculated in a couple of different ways. One is to add up all your overhead costs and divide them by the total budget. Then you would apply that percentage to all programs equally.

A sample program budget including an overhead cost rate might look like this:

### Sample Program Budget with Overhead Rate

| Expenses | |
|---|---|
| *Personnel* | |
| Assistant Executive Director (.40 FTE @ $60,000/yr.) | $ 24,000 |
| Program Director (1 FTE @ $40,000/yr.) | $ 40,000 |
| Training Coordinator (1 FTE @ $30,000/yr.) | $ 30,000 |
| Volunteer Coordinators (2 FTEs @ $30,000/yr.) | $ 60,000 |
| | **$ 154,000** |
| Fringe Benefits (@ 30%) | $ 46,200 |
| Total Personnel | **$ 200,200** |
| *Nonpersonnel* | |
| Youth Outreach Materials | $ 1,500 |
| Mentor Outreach Materials | $ 1,500 |
| Training Workbooks | $ 500 |
| Computers (2 @ $500 ea.) | $ 1,000 |
| Printers (2 @ $200 ea.) | $ 400 |
| Software Licenses | $ 300 |

## Financial Considerations

| | | |
|---|---|---|
| Internet Fees ($30/mo. for 12 mos.) | $ | 360 |
| Rent (50% space occupancy @ $1,200/mo. for 12 mos.) | $ | 7,200 |
| Utilities (50% space occupancy $200/mo. for 12 mos.) | $ | 1,200 |
| Phone ($50/mo. for 12 mos.) | $ | 600 |
| Office Supplies | $ | 1,000 |
| Classified Advertising | $ | 500 |
| Dues and Subscriptions | $ | 1,000 |
| Conferences | $ | 1,200 |
| Local Travel | $ | 250 |
| Long Distance Travel | $ | 2,400 |
| Total Nonpersonnel | $ | 20,910 |
| Total Personnel | $ | 200,200 |
| | $ | 221,110 |
| General and Administrative (10%) | $ | 22,111 |
| Total Expenses | $ | 243,221 |

A sample event budget with an overhead cost rate might look like this:

### Sample Gala Cost Budget with Overhead Rate

| Expenses | | |
|---|---|---|
| Invitation Printing | $ | 2,000 |
| Mailing | $ | 2,000 |
| Ad Journal | $ | 2,000 |
| Venue | $ | 15,000 |
| Honoree Awards | $ | 500 |
| Flowers | $ | 1,000 |
| Photographer | $ | 750 |

| Expenses | |
|---|---|
| Fundraising Coordinator (.33 FTE @ $45,000/yr.) | $ 15,000 |
| Fringe Benefits (.30 percent of salary) | $ 5,000 |
| Clerical Support (100 hours @ $15/hr.) | $ 1,500 |
| Telephone | $ 100 |
| Office Supplies (paper, printer cartridge, copying, etc.) | $ 150 |
| Total Direct Costs | $ 45,000 |
| Overhead (10%) | $ 4,500 |
| Total Event Costs | $ 49,500 |

Another way to calculate overhead expense is to add up all your overhead costs and multiply that by program percentage of budget.

In this case, both methods result in the same overhead cost rate. That isn't always the case. Either way you calculate your indirect costs, be consistent throughout all your budget calculations. Use the same formula every time. You want to be able to compare apples to apples.

---

**Sample Overhead Rate Calculation**

Program A Direct Costs: $45,000

Total Organizational Budget: $300,000

Total Organizational Overhead Expenses: $30,000

$45,000 Program A Direct Costs/$300,000 Total Organizational Budget = 0.15

$30,000 Organizational Overhead Costs x 0.15 = $4,500 Program A Overhead Allocation

**Example**

---

Whichever way you calculate indirect costs, you need to know your total costs so that you can figure out a revenue strategy. I talk about revenue strategies later in the chapter. You will also want to know your net income (how much revenue exceeds costs) to know if the event was successful, and, if so, how successful it was.

### Opportunity Costs

Opportunity costs are not costs represented in

a budget as one of its line items. Opportunity costs are more conceptual. They are the costs you incur for making certain choices over others, the costs associated with taking advantage of one opportunity over another. Opportunity costs are usually not expressed in financial terms, although the decisions relating to them will have financial implications.

For example, suppose your organization is looking for a new facility for its gala. From a financial point of view, you would find out what costs are associated with different venues, for example, plate charges, bar charges, maître d' fees, gratuity, and, if needed, valet parking costs. You'd add up all the costs associated with each facility and determine that lowest price wins.

But that's not always how the decisions are made. Sometimes you might decide to go with a higher-priced vendor because you see an opportunity to accomplish other things besides paying the lowest price. What else are you getting in return for holding your event there?

For example, what are the payment terms? Does timing of payments fit your cash-flow needs? Do you have to guarantee a certain amount when you reserve or is guaranteeing a week beforehand okay? Does the facility's management know you and your organization well so that it's easy to work with them year after year? Is your guest list growing and you need a bigger place? Do you cover a large geographic area and want to rotate where you hold the gala so that it is easier for different constituents to attend? Or do you want to be known for one location and be easy to find every year? Does the facility have a great brand in the community where association with that facility will also brand your event? In short, what are the opportunities associated with choosing one vendor over another? And do those opportunities outweigh the increased costs?

This principle can be applied to all your organizational and fundraising partnerships. For example, is the donation from that high-maintenance donor really worth it? What is that donor expecting in return? Can you really deliver? Is spending time courting one donor worth the time you could be spending on other fundraising activities?

In the same vein, is that grant with all the time-consuming reporting requirements worth it? Do you have the time or the staff to gather everything you need for that one funder or is your time better spent on other requests? What other benefits do you gain besides money in accepting that grant?

In this example, aligning ourselves with this particular agency presented opportunities that outweighed the costs. The financial analysis suggested that we forgo this funding opportunity. But our agency was not willing to forgo the other opportunities the funding offered. In this case, the financial costs associated with the opportunity for community visibility and networking opportunities were well worth the organizational investment.

In order to take advantage of one opportunity over another, weighing their costs, you must be familiar with the needs, goals, and values of your organization. All of them—not just the financial ones. That is why it is so important to be extremely familiar with your agency's strategic plan. To be able to negotiate a win-win agreement, you must know what resources you need to accomplish your goals. The great thing about partners is that they generally have many things they can bring to a relationship beyond

> I once worked with an agency that applied for a community grant from a funder. In my mind, the staff time and effort it took to prepare the application and the time it took to report on our agency's activities was not worth the money we got from the funder. When we added up the time it took the financial director to prepare the budget using the funder's forms, the time it took me to write the proposal, the time it took the program staff to gather all the statistics the way the funder wanted, and the time it took for me to attend the mandatory quarterly meetings—and translated all those time costs into dollars—clearly we were spending more money than we were taking in.
>
> But being funded by this particular funder brought credibility to our agency among other funders, enhanced community visibility, and let us rub shoulders with important community decision-makers. For us, the opportunities the funder provided were worth the extra costs associated with the application and reporting requirements.
>
> **stories from the real world**

what you are initially looking for. And your organization probably has more of value to bring to the partnership than you might first think.

## Net Income

You must calculate your expenses to ensure that your revenues will cover them. You need to at least break even. The name of the game is not increased revenues. The name of the game is increased net income, that is, revenue minus expenses. If you don't generate enough net income, you will go out of business. Then where will your mission be?

> I once worked for an organization where we were looking for the best deal we could find on mortgages. I had developed a relationship with a local bank, and the president was willing to meet with me and the executive director. My goal was to get the lowest below-market interest rate possible.
>
> My executive director, though, settled on an interest rate a full percentage point above what I thought we could ask for. When I asked why, he told me that he didn't want to bleed the bank. He wanted to be able to go back for additional financing as we expanded our real-estate portfolio. The executive director felt that the ability to go back to the bank again and again was worth the cost of settling at the higher interest rate.
>
> **stories from the real world**

Notice in this formula there are only two ways to increase net income: increase revenues and/or decrease expenses. I talked about ways to increase revenues and reduce expenses in **Chapter Three**.

I also talked about ways to increase gross revenues: increase volume, increase price, or a combination of the two. I talked about ways to increase volume in **Chapter Three**. Here I'll talk about pricing strategies.

> The strategic plan is a good place to start to determine what you can offer to a partner and what you need to receive.
>
> **food for thought**

### Market-Based Pricing

One way to price goods or services is to charge whatever your market will bear. This means knowing what your market is, who else is in your market, and what others are charging for their goods and services. It means knowing your buyer, as well as your consumer. They might not be the same groups of people. In many nonprofits, the people who consume the goods or services are not the same people who pay for them. Often a foundation, corporation, government, or individual donor actually pays for, or finances, the provision of a nonprofit's goods or services. For example, colleges have scholarships that pay for students to attend there: it is the student who receives the education but it is the scholarship donor who pays for it, or part of it. People who are homeless use the services of a homeless shelter, but the government or other funders pay for it. The point is that when an organization considers its pricing structure, it needs to be aware that its consumers and its buyers might be two different markets.

> **Sample Net Income Calculation**
>
> Total Revenues: $300,000
>
> Total Expenses: $275,000
>
> $300,000 Total Revenues −
> $275,000 Total Expenses =
> $25,000 Net Income
>
> **Example**

Knowing what the market will bear requires research. This is where industry and professional associations help. At least with a larger pool of organizations, you can get a feel for what others are charging for their services, and it doesn't cost you much to find out, except for time and maybe a membership fee. There are also more formal ways to conduct market research, but most nonprofits don't have many resources devoted to marketing.

Of course, you have to calculate net income to see whether the market price covers all your program's expenses. And if it doesn't, you either find some way to subsidize the service or you don't provide it. Either way, you need to do an analysis *before* you take on a project. The last thing you want to do is take on something that will put your organization's viability in jeopardy.

For example, if your program is projected to have total costs of $300,000, you had better be able to develop partnerships that raise at least $300,000 in revenues. Suppose it costs you $300,000 to function as an organization.

Your government funders are only willing to pay $150,000 of those costs. You need to make up your loss in net income in other ways. You need to structure your revenue streams so that you cover the other $150,000 in expenses. One revenue structure might look like this:

## Sample $300,000 Program Revenue Structure

| Revenues | |
|---|---|
| Government Contract | $ 150,000 |
| Special Events | $ 75,000 |
| Foundations | $ 50,000 |
| Individual Donations | $ 25,000 |
| Total Revenues | $ 300,000 |
| Total Expenses | $ 300,000 |
| Net Income | $ 0 |

In this example, the nonprofit breaks even. The agency must meet its budgeted revenue goals or its viability is in jeopardy. This puts a lot of pressure on the development staff. And it means that the agency needs a backup plan in case it doesn't meet its revenue goals through its other funding partnerships.

Government contracts are usually awarded on market-based pricing. Funding agencies know how much it costs to run a program, and they use that information to set their contract amounts. Foundations are also generally familiar with what other similar programs cost to run. Expenses above or below that range might cause them to question your organization's operational effectiveness.

### *Profit-Based Pricing*

Special events, though, usually utilize a combination of profit-based and market-based pricing structures.

For example, if your gala is projected to have total costs of $44,000, you will need to raise at least $44,000 in revenues to break even. But the point of many special events is to make money, so prices are usually way above the actual expense incurred. So a dinner might cost your organization $50 a plate while you charge $150 per ticket. The price of the ticket is set according to how much profit you want to take in.

But you do don't want to price yourself out of the market. Your gala ticket will probably fall into a range comparable to what other nonprofits are charging for similar galas. So your ticket price is also influenced by market factors.

Gala sponsorships operate the same way. You know you much profit you want to make, but your pricing structure is influenced by how much the market will bear.

One revenue structure may look like this:

### Sample Gala Revenue Structure #1

| Revenues | |
|---|---|
| 1 Sponsorship @ $5,000 | $ 5,000 |
| 2 Sponsorships @ $2,500 | $ 5,000 |
| 3 Sponsorships @ $1,000 | $ 3,000 |
| 4 Full-Page Journal Ads @ $500 | $ 2,000 |
| 6 ½-Page Journal Ads @ $250 | $ 1,500 |
| 8 ¼-Page Journal Ads @ $100 | $ 800 |
| 100 Tickets @ $150 each | $ 15,000 |
| Silent Auction | $ 5,000 |
| Total Revenues | $ 37,300 |
| Total Expenses | $ 44,000 |
| Net Income | $ (6,700) |

In this example, gala revenues do not cover total expenses. The organization will lose money if it implements this revenue structure. To rectify the problem, the organization can increase the price of its sponsorships and ads, pursue a greater number of sponsorships or ads, or add another product such as a live auction or raffle.

An adjusted revenue structure may look like this:

## Sample Gala Revenue Structure #2

| Revenues | |
|---|---|
| 1 Sponsorship @ $5,000 | $ 5,000 |
| 1 Sponsorship @ $3,500 | $ 3,500 |
| 3 Sponsorships @ $2,500 | $ 7,500 |
| 4 Sponsorships @ $1,250 | $ 5,000 |
| 4 Full-Page Journal Ads @ $650 | $ 2,600 |
| 6 ½-Page Journal Ads @ $400 | $ 2,400 |
| 8 ¼-Page Journal Ads @ $250 | $ 2,000 |
| 8 Business cards Ads @ $75 | $ 600 |
| 10 Listings @ $25 | $ 250 |
| 100 Tickets @ $175 each | $ 17,500 |
| Silent Auction | $ 5,000 |
| 50/50 Raffle | $ 750 |
| Total Revenues | $ 52,100 |
| Total Expenses | $ 44,000 |
| Net Income | $ 8,100 |

Notice that in addition to a more robust pricing structure, I have added to the number of sponsorships and ads needed, and also increased the price of the tickets. If you make changes like this, you better leave enough time to get to know the needs of your corporate market and build solid relationships with corporate donors. And you better know the needs and preferences of your attendee market too. Just because you put a line item in a budget doesn't mean it will happen. It takes time to build these types of partnerships.

It is important to consider your total costs along with your revenue strategies, so you know how much to ask for, can target your asks, and can generate enough revenue to stay in business. Raising lots of money means knowing how much you need to raise and what types of revenue you need to go after. It determines which partnerships you will spend your time developing.

## To Recap

◆ Take into account *all* direct and indirect costs when determining your budget.

◆ Weigh your opportunity costs.

◆ Ensure positive net income.

◆ Know what prices your consumer *and* buyer markets will bear.

◆ Develop partnerships that enhance your pricing strategies.

# Chapter Seven

## Ensuring Maximum Profit

### IN THIS CHAPTER

- Considering return on investment
- Profit margin
- Managing cash flow

Profit? What do I mean profit? Even the name, nonprofit, says we don't make profits.

The word "nonprofit" is an unfortunate misnomer. Making a profit, by definition, is simply taking in more revenues than laying out expenses, i.e., realizing a positive net income. Nonprofits *can* make a profit. They just have to reinvest the profit back into the organization as opposed to distributing it to individual company owners. In fact, a nonprofit *must* make a profit if it is to grow.

In this chapter, I discuss how to determine the optimal allocation of resources needed to generate different levels of income. I talk about return on investment, resource efficiency, and cash-flow considerations. I define these terms as we go along. For a more complete discussion of these concepts, see my book *Succeed in Your Nonprofit Funding Partnerships: Analyzing Their Costs and Benefits*.

## Return on Investment

Return on investment is a measure of how well your financial investments are performing for you. By financial investment, I mean the value of all the resources it takes to achieve a certain outcome. In other words, return on investment tells you in financial terms how effective your allocation of resources is.

Return on investment is expressed by a percentage or ratio. It is calculated by subtracting total costs from total revenues and dividing the result by total costs. For example:

> **Sample Return on Investment**
>
> Total Revenues = $300,000
>
> Total Expenses = $275,000
>
> (Total Revenues − Total Expenses)/Total Expenses = Return on Investment
>
> ($300,000 − $275,000)/$275,000 = Return on Investment
>
> $25,000/$275,000 = 0.09 = 9 percent
>
> **Example**

A 9 percent return on investment means that for every dollar you spend, you get $1.09 in return.

Return on investment can be used to an organization's marketing advantage. A high return on investment will make your organization attractive to partners who want to leverage their investments.

In the last chapter, I talked a lot about total costs and their importance in calculating true net income. In order to calculate return on investment, you must also calculate total revenues—cash and noncash. Here is where the financial value of volunteer time and in-kind contributions comes into play. I talked about volunteer and in-kind contributions in **Chapter Three**.

> I currently work for an organization that is mainly staffed by volunteers. Once I take into account the value of the volunteer hours as part of revenue, my organization's return on investment goes through the roof. My organization is very attractive to donors of all kinds.
>
> **stories from the real world**

Return on investment can be not only an important marketing tool; it can also help you make decisions regarding the best type of fundraising partnerships to pursue.

For example, say that you implement a gala, conduct an annual appeal, and write grants. Suppose that you hired a grants writer for $40,000 a year to raise $100,000, for a net income of $60,000. The annual gala costs you $45,000 to implement in total expenses (including staff time), and you realize total revenues of $65,000, for a net income of $20,000. The annual appeal costs you, including staff time, $1,800 to implement and raises you $10,000, for a net income of $8,200. Which activity should you invest your time in growing?

> **Sample Comparative Return on Investment**
>
> Grant Funding: $60,000 Net Income / $40,000 Expenses = 1.5 or 150 percent Grant Funding Return on Investment
>
> Gala: $20,000 Net Income / $45,000 Expenses = 0.44 or 44 percent Gala Return on Investment
>
> Annual Appeal: $8,500 Net Income / $1,800 Expenses = 4.72 or 472 percent Annual Appeal Return on Investment
>
> **Example**

One way is to compare your different rates of return on investment.

If you are looking for the most financial leverage for your dollar, it will be to your advantage to grow your annual appeal and grants activities as opposed to your gala. Knowing this information tells you where to spend your time developing what partnerships. I talked about identifying partners in **Chapter One**, building relationships with them in **Chapter Two**, and reaching them in **Chapter Four**.

Calculate the return on investment for all your different fundraising activities and see what you get. You will probably find out that, even though special events are a favorite way for nonprofits to raise money, their return on investment is low compared to other forms of fundraising.

> I once worked for an organization with a 65 percent staff turnover rate. To compensate, this organization had to invest heavily in constant recruitment and training activities. The high turnover also caused a lack of continuity in service delivery, which decreased client satisfaction. A better investment in improving staff morale would have more than paid back costs associated with the turnover, the agency's effectiveness would have skyrocketed, and their already good brand would have become even more valuable.
>
> **stories from the real world**

Of course, financial return on investment is not the only type of return worth considering. Other types may be just as important to your organization. For example, that big gala may raise your organization's visibility in the community and lend to your agency's brand. Or it may build a stronger relationship with an honoree. Or you might use your gala as a point of entry for other potential donors; the gala may be intentionally designed to be a cultivation event.

There are many nonfinancial reasons why your organization might choose to invest resources into an activity with low financial return on investment. The point is, make these decisions intentionally, with forethought and planning.

Return on investment can also be applied internally. Your organization may be able to reduce expenses and improve return on investment by paying attention to its partnership with its employees.

## Profit Margin

To determine profit margin, divide net income by total revenues. Profit margin tells you the percentage of

---

**Sample Profit Margin**

(Total Revenues – Total Expenses) / Total Revenues = Profit Margin

($300,000 Total Revenues – $275,000 Total Expenses) / $300,000 Total Revenues = Profit Margin

$25,000/$300,000 = 0.083 = 8.3 percent

**Example**

your revenues that is not allocated to costs. The higher your profit margin, the more efficiently you use the resources you have in providing your goods and services.

In the example of how to calculate profit margin, this organization realizes an 8.3 percent profit margin, or, in other words, 91.7 percent of revenue is used to generate the organization's goods and services and 8.3 percent of revenue is profit.

As you can see, return on investment is highly related to profit margin. Whereas return on investment tells you where you get the greatest return on your use of resources, profit margin tells you how efficiently those resources are being used in generating your profit. Both are useful ratios.

## Cash Flow

When I was a development director, I cared most about revenues. Expenses were tangential, except as they related to how much revenue I needed to generate. For grant funding, I also cared about when my revenues came in so that I knew how to schedule my program operations and when my programs could start. But generating revenue was mostly my world. Cash flow was something I really didn't worry about.

As an executive director, I am as concerned about cash flow as generating revenues. Managing when revenues come in with when cash goes out is a lot harder than it sounds.

It is important to consider when money comes in and when it is going out, so you can plan accordingly. Your organization needs to realize enough revenues to cover expenses when they are due or it will go out of business. If you are responsible for revenue generation, you better time the revenues coming in with the expenses going out. Cash flow, then, has implications for when you implement your fundraising activities.

> According to recent GuideStar organizational surveys, 46 percent of survey participants said that their organizations receive the bulk of their contributions in the last quarter of the year.
>
> **observation**

There are many reasons why the revenues coming in might not line up with when the cash needs to go out. Your organization might be paid on a reimbursement basis. Or your organization might be government funded, and the government might be late in making payments. Or a significant portion of your revenue might come when you hold an event or conduct an appeal. Or foundation revenue might come in all at once. At the same time, many of your organization's expenses are probably pretty steady, such as personnel, office supplies, Internet, phone, rent, and utilities. Although you might have a positive net income at the end of a year, your cash flow from month to month might or might not be positive.

A cash-flow analysis is extremely useful to project which months your organization will have a surplus of revenues and which months a surplus of expenses. A cash-flow analysis is a month-by-month projection of when revenues and expenses will be realized and how much net income is realized each month. For those months where expenses exceed revenues, you tap into the reserves created by the months when revenues exceed expenses.

A sample cash-flow analysis is on the facing page:

## Sample Cash Flow Projection #1 (in 000's)

| | Budget | Jan | Feb | Mar | Apr | May | Jun | Jul | Aug | Sep | Oct | Nov | Dec |
|---|---|---|---|---|---|---|---|---|---|---|---|---|---|
| **Revenues** | | | | | | | | | | | | | |
| Government | 120 | 10 | 10 | 10 | 10 | 10 | 10 | 10 | 10 | 10 | 10 | 10 | 10 |
| Foundations | 50 | 5 | 0 | 0 | 5 | 5 | 0 | 0 | 5 | 5 | 5 | 5 | 15 |
| Corporate Giving | 10 | 0 | 0 | 0 | 0 | 5 | 0 | 0 | 0 | 0 | 0 | 0 | 5 |
| Gala | 50 | 0 | 0 | 0 | 0 | 0 | 0 | 0 | 5 | 15 | 30 | 0 | 0 |
| Annual Appeal | 25 | 5 | 0 | 0 | 0 | 0 | 0 | 0 | 0 | 0 | 0 | 0 | 20 |
| Major Gifts | 45 | 0 | 0 | 0 | 5 | 5 | 5 | 0 | 0 | 0 | 0 | 10 | 20 |
| Total Revenues | 300 | 20 | 10 | 10 | 20 | 25 | 15 | 10 | 20 | 30 | 45 | 25 | 70 |
| **Expenses** | | | | | | | | | | | | | |
| Operating | (230) | (22) | (18) | (18) | (19) | (19) | (18) | (18) | (18) | (20) | (20) | (20) | (20) |
| Fundraising | (45) | (3) | (3) | (3) | (4) | (3) | (3) | (3) | (3) | (4) | (5) | (8) | (3) |
| Total Expenses | (275) | (25) | (21) | (21) | (23) | (22) | (21) | (21) | (21) | (25) | (25) | (28) | (23) |
| Net Income | 25 | (5) | (11) | (11) | (3) | 3 | (6) | (11) | (1) | 6 | 20 | (3) | 47 |
| Account Balance | 25 | 20 | 9 | (2) | (5) | (2) | (8) | (19) | (20) | (14) | 6 | 3 | 50 |

Ensuring Maximum Profit 95

In this example, this organization has a revenue mix that includes government, foundation, corporate, special event, annual appeal, and major gift funding for total revenues of $300,000. The government funding is expected to be continuous while the others come in at different times of the year.

Expenses are projected at $275,000 and are much more stable over time. The spikes in operating expenses may be attributable to higher utility costs, timing of conference registrations and travel, or one-time expenses such as staff memberships and journals. The spikes in fundraising expenses correspond to when costs for the gala and annual appeal occur.

Notice how the monthly net income in this budget fluctuates. Even though this organization has a positive net income at the end of the year, only five of the seven months show a positive net income.

This income fluctuation has serious implications for cash flow. Assuming the organization starts with a $25,000 account balance, the account is in a negative balance from March to August. No organization can survive with this kind of cash flow. The organization must either start with a bigger account balance, step up fundraising activities so that more revenue is achieved earlier in the year, or consider loan options such as a line of credit or mission-related investments.

The point here is that the timing of your partnerships matters. It is important for you or someone else in your organization to have a finger on the pulse of the cash flow.

Return on investment and profit margins are important to take into

> **definition**
>
> A mission-related investment, sometimes referred to as a program-related investment, is a hybrid combination of a grant and a loan. Mission-related investments are loans from foundations where the loan is given at a far-below market rate. As a loan, it is expected to be paid back according to a legal agreement. As a significantly below-market-rate loan, although it needs to be repaid, the loan is considered by the IRS to be a charitable gift and counts toward the charitable distributions foundations are required to make. Mission-related investments are most often given as loans, loan guarantees, or lines of credit.

account when you are weighing one option against another. Cash flow is important in determining when funding partnerships need to come to fruition. All of these factors are important to setting the goals you want to achieve from a particular partnership and establishing the parameters of your negotiating stance during partnership formation.

## To Recap

- ◆ Calculate return on investment to see how much your resources are leveraged.

- ◆ Determine profit margin to see how much of your revenue is tied up in costs.

- ◆ Keep a close eye on cash flow and time your partnerships accordingly.

# Chapter Eight

## Making the Deal

**IN THIS CHAPTER**

- The importance of formulating overarching goals
- Implementing fair process
- The basis of fair outcomes
- Ethical considerations
- When the partnership doesn't work

Now that you know who your potential partners are, what their interests are in interacting with you, and the specific returns you will realize if you engage in a partnership with them, it is time to negotiate what that partnership will look like. To succeed, each party engaging in the partnership must come out of the deal feeling as though they are gaining something of value. The more people, or entities, that are involved in the partnership, the more complicated the negotiations.

### Formulating Overarching Goals

Overarching goals are goals that supersede each party's specific interests, perspectives, and organizational cultures. They are not based solely on what you want out of the partnership—they go beyond your organization's wants and needs. Neither are they based solely on the other parties' wants and needs. Overarching goals encompass the needs of all the parties.

Which is why connecting on values works so well. What a party is trying to accomplish and how it accomplishes it is, as we have seen, a values proposition. Understanding and stating those values puts the conversation on a different level. A common value will help you overcome differences in method and culture, as I talked about in **Chapter Five**.

Formulating overarching goals means that you need to thoroughly know your own organization and what is important to it. You will be making values decisions and you need to know your organization's values like the back of your hand. In **Chapter One**, I talked about familiarity with your organization's strategic plan and values as a basis for identifying potential partners.

Familiarity with the organizational strategic plan and values is also crucial to your negotiating position. To come out with something of value to your organization, you must know what your organization values and the degrees of value any one component has.

Formulating overarching goals also means you thoroughly know your potential partners and what they value. In **Chapter Two**, I talked about listening to and building relationships with potential partners.

It is important to start discussions with potential partners by exploring common values, so you can set a precedent of agreement right off the starting block. People feel most comfortable with people who they think are like them. You want to show that you have things in common with them, that you are not an outsider who doesn't understand. Shared values show your commonality. You become one of the gang as opposed to a complete outsider.

And it is important that all parties come to agreement around common goals. Partnerships are really a series of small agreements. One of the first things you all need to agree on is why you are there, why everyone is investing their time in interacting with one another. Oftentimes, people assume they know why people are interested in partnering with them. Don't do that. You never know people's motivations, and people do things for different reasons. Your job in getting to know people is to understand what those motivations are. A partnership starts with agreeing on what all parties are trying to accomplish. You will waste your time if everyone does not start out on the same page.

It is also important that all parties come to agreement around common goals so that everyone gets used to coming to agreement. Agreement right off the bat about why you are all there sets good precedent. Even if your group is only a duo, you will be making a series of small agreements to meet your end goal. Start out with a win. Start out with an atmosphere of agreement. Start out agreeing on common goals.

> One of the accomplishments I am most proud of during the course of my career was the formation of a statewide advisory committee involving a number of organizations that didn't always get along. One statewide agency represented a teacher's union, another the state's educational department, and the third a parent constituency group. The number of lawsuits flying among the groups was dizzying.
>
> But, we were all interested in providing a good educational start to the children in the state. We agreed that we would work together in our different roles toward that one goal: improved school readiness. School readiness and the wellbeing of the children superseded all of the issues between the groups and they realized that by working together they had a chance to make a real difference.
>
> We were an effective group that worked well together once we defined and stated what our purpose for being was and what the ground rules were for interacting with one another. We stated our common goals and values and superseded our differences.
>
> **stories from the real world**

## Ensuring Fairness

When in negotiations, each party must feel that they are treated fairly, or else the negotiation doesn't work. People need to feel they are not being taken advantage of. They want to feel valued throughout the process and with the outcome.

### *Fair Process*

An often overlooked potential point of agreement is that of the process the negotiations themselves will take. There are many points of the process that can and should be agreed upon both to make the negotiations themselves go more smoothly and to continue your precedence of coming to agreement.

Someone needs to take the lead in a group. In complicated negotiations, this can be a judge or an arbitrator. If you are in funding negotiations that require this level of third-party interaction, you are probably entangled in a legal dispute stemming from a partnership that was ill-defined or has gone bad. I'll talk about dealing with partnerships gone bad later in this chapter.

Most likely, the group leader will be someone in the group. All parties in the negotiation must agree on who this person will be. This person's responsibilities might include things like developing and sticking to the agenda. In larger groups or longer negotiations, written agendas and minutes are a good idea. They keep everyone on the same page without veering from the topic. In smaller groups or shorter negotiations, you will still need an agenda, but it will probably be oral rather than written. For example, the leader saying something like: "Thank you for meeting with me. I wanted to meet with you to talk about …." However you end up doing it, you want to provide the structure to help everyone stay on track.

A good practice is to gain agreement on the agenda before delving into it. Saying something like, "Is that okay with you?" or, "Is that your understanding as well?" goes a long way. That way, if someone else has a different agenda or a different understanding of the agenda, you can address the issue. (Notice the use of the feedback loop. I discussed the importance of the feedback loop in **Chapter Two**.)

Once you have agreement on an agenda, it should be relatively easy to stick to it. If discussions get off track, just call parties back to what was agreed on in the first place.

Once you and your partners all agree on what you want to accomplish, you need agreement on when you plan to accomplish it. For meetings, that means coming to agreement about when meetings will take place, how long the meetings will last, and the agenda. For contributions, that means coming to agreement on when the gift will be given and over what period of time. For example, is the whole amount going to be paid at once or over a period of time? At what intervals? And when will your partners start realizing what they expect from the deal?

Agreement on process is especially important when cultivating donors, particularly major donors. A major gift ask usually requires a series of interactions. You need agreement on when you'll meet, where you'll meet, what the goal of the meeting is, and who the participants in the meeting are. Once there, you will need to establish an agenda and ask for agreement on that. After the meeting, you will need agreement on whether you'll meet again. Ultimately, you will need agreement on the amount of the gift, the timing of the gift, and the form that gift will take.

Skip any one of these steps and you might jeopardize your relationship with the donor and risk receipt of the gift.

**practical tip**

Don't assume anything. Everything needs to be discussed. And agreed upon. I have seen negotiations fall apart after agreement on outcome because process was never discussed and became an issue. Don't let that happen to you.

*stories from the real world*

I regularly partner with for-profit companies for their marketing expertise. We both receive value from the improved exposure we get in the community. I value the opportunity to improve my corporate image and communications. They value having their name associated with a charitable cause as it improves their bottom line. To me, the marketing expertise is worth it. To them, the volunteer hours are worth it. We both win.

### Fair Outcome

Fair outcome is what most people think of when they think about coming to an agreement. Outcome is what both parties walk away with. For a partnership to last, as you want with fundraising partnerships, all parties need to walk away feeling that they got one in the win column. You need to structure a win-win outcome for all involved.

Which is why negotiating from a values standpoint is so powerful. If you know what is important to your partners, and you can give them or help them get some of that, you can create a win for them. And they for you.

Values cannot be monetized. How important is it to you and your partners that your respective missions be fulfilled? Priceless. You need resources to make your organization run, but the resources themselves are not what you are ultimately after. It is keeping someone safe, making sure someone gets a healthy meal, providing clean water to drink, or whatever your mission is. It is fulfilling your mission that is important—money is just a vehicle to do it.

Values, then, are a great equalizer. It doesn't matter how big your organization's budget is, or how many staff it has, or how long it's been around, as long as it can contribute to fulfillment of the values important to its partners. You don't need to compete with one another. When you negotiate on the basis of values, the power relationship between the partners is equalized. You are all gaining something you value.

Negotiating on values allows you and your partners as a group to think outside the box, for solutions that none of you could come up with alone. That's because values are not method-bound. Values fulfillment is not necessarily through money. There are many ways to fulfill a value.

> Once I was part of a group consisting of a very young residential youth organization with a large budget, a very old counseling organization with a medium-sized budget, and a court-advocacy organization that had been around for a medium length of time and had a very small budget. We were trying to put together a program for at-risk youth who had aged out of the foster-care system. We forged the partnership because together we could offer a broader array of services at less cost than we could individually.
>
> We were all equal in terms of what we could offer the partnership, even though we came together with different organizational ages and budgets. The agency with the large budget had entrée to at-risk youth who had aged out as well as a solid accounting department. The agency with the medium-sized budget had the clinical expertise needed to make the project work. And the agency with the small budget had access to a large volunteer base to act as mentors.
>
> **stories from the real world**

For example, in **Chapter Five**, I gave the example of my organization's partnership with the business community around the issue of safety. If I had gone into the partnership negotiation looking for money, I would not have gotten very far. Money would have become the issue, rather than the safety of our clients. Focusing on safety brought me so much more than money. I got my mission promoted to a constituency I would not have otherwise, I addressed community concerns, raised my organizational visibility, and I got advocates for legislation that was important to me. I promoted mission in a way far more valuable than a few thousand dollars could.

Funding partnerships, then, can be about more than just money. They are about organizational visibility and branding. They are about engaging people in your cause beyond the donation. In fact, a donation is often the result of a person already engaged with your organization. I talked about identifying these types of partners in **Chapter One**.

If you do the work to prepare for your negotiations—identifying potential partners; building relationships; listening to their needs, desires, and motivations—you will be able to deliver a win for your partners. You will know them and what is important to them. If you also know what is important to your organization, have a variety of ways that others can contribute to you, and have considered the financial factors involved, you will be able to structure an agreement that is a win for your organization.

## Ethical Considerations

In your negotiations in setting up a partnership, it is extremely important that you are ethical and above reproach. That means that you are truthful and honest in what you say and what you promise. Don't overstate or understate the facts to better position your agency. Let the facts be the facts, whatever they might be.

That doesn't mean that you need to reveal everything. If you're asked, of course, be truthful. But if you are not asked, you don't need to answer. For example, remember in **Chapter Seven** the example of the organization with the 65 percent turnover rate? That agency also had only a 5 percent vacancy rate, that is, only 5 percent of all staff positions were unfilled at any one time. The industry rate was a 25 percent vacancy rate. We had also gained high accreditation scores for our pursuit of excellence. You can bet that when I wanted to position our agency as a leader in the field, I talked about that low 5 percent vacancy rate as opposed to the high turnover rate. When asked about staff turnover rates, I was always truthful. As part of the conversation, though, I always pointed to our low vacancy rate as well as our high job-performance standards.

Don't overpromise or try to make yourself or your organization bigger than it is. The last thing you want to do is enter into a partnership promising a certain outcome or return without being able to deliver. Not good for your branding. Once you or your organization get a reputation in the community, it is very difficult to change it. You do not want a reputation for not being able to deliver, or worse, for being prone to misrepresent yourself. Only promise what you can reasonably deliver.

> It is especially crucial to grantor-grantee relationships and other designated-gifts relationships to notify funders immediately if there are changes in scope or timing of your agreed-upon outcomes. Grant funding and gifts designated for certain uses are bound by the objectives and purposes described by the donor or in the proposal application. The designation set forth by the donor or the proposal and any approved revisions to the original agreements are legal documents with legal liabilities attached to them.
> 
> 👍 practical tip

Of course, sometimes the unexpected happens and you are not able to fulfill your promises. In those cases, it is important that you notify your partners immediately to let them know that you will not be able to hold up your end of the bargain as agreed. Perhaps that will nullify the partnership. Or perhaps that will lead to more negotiations. Whatever the outcome, it is important for you to maintain your organization's credibility. Admit and correct your mistakes, especially as they affect the partnerships you have developed.

Be consistent in all you say and do. Don't tell one partner one thing and another something else. And don't change your story from one partnership to the next. Let people get to know you and your organization. Build a relationship with them and let them build a relationship with you. Let the partnerships you most value go deep. Be transparent and be consistent. People need to know what they can expect from you.

Stay true to your organization's mission. No matter how lucrative a partnership may seem, if it doesn't fit your mission, don't do it. Only engage in those partnerships that will promote and enhance your mission.

If your organization starts to engage in activities that do not promote your mission, your organization will experience mission drift. This often happens to nonprofits that are in dire need of money or are having a cash-flow crunch. They start chasing the money as opposed to fulfilling the mission. Sooner or later the organization becomes so involved in revenue-generation activities above mission-related activities, that they are no longer defined by their mission. The organization loses its identity and might, depending on the activities, be in danger of losing its tax-exempt status. Dire consequences to pay. Always stick to the mission.

> **watch out!** Be aware of the tax laws relating to mission-related income and unrelated business income.

Above all, stay true to your organization's values. Don't ever compromise your values. Sometimes this means not participating in or perhaps giving up a partnership, even if the partnership is lucrative. Maintaining your values is much more important than money. Maintain integrity. Live up to your values. Be known for how you conduct yourself as well as the goods or services your agency delivers.

Many professions maintain a code of ethics which members must abide by. This holds true for fundraising too. If you are a fundraising professional, I suggest you become familiar with the Association of Fundraising Professionals Code of Ethical Principles and Standards. In addition, if you are a grant writer, I suggest the Grant Professionals Association Code of Ethics. (Both can be found in the appendixes.)

## When the Partnership Doesn't Work

Sometimes partnerships just don't work. They seem like a good fit, they were worth exploring, but things just aren't going to work out.

It is important that you know when to walk away from a partnership or partnership negotiations. Sometimes people become so focused on the goal of forming a new partnership that it becomes all-consuming. Or they really like the people involved in the partnerships. Or they want to prove themselves. Or whatever. In any case, you need to know at what point you are going to walk away.

You know it is time to walk away from a partnership when the benefits are less than the costs. I talked about determining financial and opportunity costs in **Chapter Six**. I talked about how to ensure profit in **Chapter Seven**.

No matter how many contingencies you might have built into the partnership agreement, sometimes something unexpected happens and you need to walk away. It is important, in these cases, to have an exit strategy built into the agreement. Include in your agreement what will happen if one or more of you decide to leave the partnership. Always have an out for your organization in case the unexpected happens.

Always have an exit strategy and contingency plan in case things don't work out.

Formulating overarching goals can bring disparate partners together. Overarching goals supersede any one party's interests. The most all-

> Partnerships dissolve all the time. I once worked with a small agency that was looking at partnering with a statewide nonprofit. The partnership would expand the reach of the smaller agency and, just as importantly, bring much needed resources to the agency, which was struggling financially. The partnership would also expand the programmatic offerings of the statewide nonprofit. Promising negotiations went on for a few months and everyone was ecstatic that the partnership seemed to be coming to fruition.
>
> But then the executive director of the statewide nonprofit left his organization. Negotiations suddenly stopped. The smaller agency turned to a related entity to try to partner on a smaller scale but that didn't work out either.
>
> The smaller agency was left in the lurch. Since negotiations with the statewide agency were going so well, they had not made a crisis contingency plan. The smaller agency was stuck having to scramble with making last-minute, unplanned decisions.
>
> **stories from the real world**

encompassing goals are based on shared organizational values. Come to agreement on those values. To keep the momentum of agreement going, agree on process as well as goals. Include agendas and time frames.

Base your outcomes on participants' values and their ability to meet the mission. Be ethical and above reproach in all your partnership activities. And, in case it doesn't work, know at what point you need to walk away. Have an exit strategy for unforeseen situations that might arise.

**To Recap**

- ◆ Formulate and agree on overarching goals.

- ◆ Agree on and implement fair processes.

- ◆ Base outcomes on values fulfillment.

- ◆ Be ethical in your negotiations and partnerships.

- ◆ Have an exit strategy and know when to walk away.

# Chapter Nine

## Maintaining the Partnership

### IN THIS CHAPTER

- Do what you say and say what you do
- Keep partners informed, especially in times of change
- Follow through
- Periodically reassess costs and benefits

To last, partnerships need to be maintained. As we have seen in **Chapter Two**, fundraisers in the United States do not do a good job of maintaining funding partnerships. So what do you need to do to make sure that you have a partner actively engaged with and giving to you year after year?

### Do What You Say and Say What You Do

When you ask for a gift, you are asking for a reason. If you are doing your job most effectively, that reason is mission related. You will be asking your partners to join you in feeding so many people, or giving so many people a home, or providing comfort and hope to so many people. Whatever your mission is, you are asking your partner to invest in your mission.

Your obligation to them is to tell them what you did with their gift or, in other words, what return they are getting on their investment. Tell them how many people you helped because of their additional gift. Or, if the gift results in a reduction in expenses, tell them how many more people you were able to help because of those cost reductions. Just like a financial firm tells its investors how their investments are doing, tell your funding partners how their investments are doing. Study after study has shown that people want to know how their gifts were used. They want to be part of your organization's success. Tell them how they were. Although this may seem simple, few organizations do this.

And tell them more than once. The thank-you letter is not enough. Do you list your accomplishments on your website? Do you give updates on projects in your newsletter? Do you give updates on progress at meetings and events? Do you have separate appreciation events for current donors and volunteers? Do you call your long-time donors and let them know the impact their gift has made over the years? Do you publish an annual report that you send to all your contributors? Through whatever channels your organization has, each touch point provides an opportunity to thank your contributors and let them know how their gifts are being used.

Notice that I am talking here about meeting mission-related needs, not organizational needs. It does not matter to donors how much money you made, how many staff members you could hire, or what expenses you

> When I ask for donations, I always relate them to mission. For example, to get the phone bill paid, I don't talk about our telephone costs. I talk instead about how $10 supports one person in crisis by keeping the lines open. Instead of staff support costs, I talk about $20 supporting one hour of volunteer training so that someone is always at the other end of the line.
>
> To let donors know how their donations are used, I talk about how many callers we had and the number of volunteer hours put in for the year. I promote how many people found comfort and hope by having a line to someone there. I use these mission-related facts in all my asks and thank-you letters, in our marketing materials, through our website, in my special-event speeches, at our appreciation events, and in our newsletter. People know where their donation is going and how it is being used.
>
> **stories from the real world**

paid, except as it relates to mission. It is *not* your organization that your donors are supporting—it is the fulfillment of your mission that they are supporting. There is a huge difference.

## Keep Them Informed

In the same vein, keep your partners informed of any progress or setbacks in the partnership. Things change. You might have new leadership, there might be a change in regulations, or you might have added other partners. Anything is possible.

Your partnership exists in the context of your changing environment, as I talked about in **Chapter Five**. Your partners are vested in how you fare in changing environments because they want to know that you can live up to your side of the bargain. How are you going to manage meeting their needs when the context of an existing partnership changes?

This is yet another reason why knowing your partners' values and basing your partnership on shared values works so well. There are many ways to

> I once formed a community network partnership with area businesses. I communicated regularly with network members, whether there were changes to the environment or not. People got accustomed to my regular updates. When changes occurred, whether they affected my organization positively or negatively, I let my partners know immediately. And they responded.
>
> One of the objectives of the organization I worked for was affordable housing. And the organization was aggressively adding to its inventory of housing while the real-estate market was down. As we added houses, I would celebrate that success with network members. I also asked for donations to move people into those houses. Some network members gave us good deals on loans, some offered to use their network to increase donations of housewares and décor, and some gave financial donations. As we used the recession to our advantage and communicated our response to that change in environment, we were able to leverage our existing partnerships to accomplish even more.

**stories from the real world**

fulfill a value. Fulfilling a value is not method-bound. And you will not have changed your mission, just your method of meeting it in accordance with the demands of a changing environment. Method is negotiable. Mission and values are not.

When the environment changes, keep all partners in the loop. Keep them close. They will help you weather whatever changes in the environment you face. You will be facing them together. Your partners care about your success as they want to realize positive return on the partnership. Use your partners when you need them.

Keep up those active listening and relationship-building skills that got you the partnership in the first place. Sometimes your partners' needs change. Listen to them and respond to their changing needs. Continually use the feedback loop. Don't necessarily assume that things are the same way they were in the past. Let your partners know you understand them. Build that relationship with them.

## Follow Through, Follow Through, Follow Through

Nothing builds trust like reliability and dependability. If you want to maintain strong partnerships, be dependable and reliable. Follow up on your promises. Don't bite off more than you can chew. Be realistic. For example, if you promise to get back to someone by a certain date, get back to them by that date. If you promise to do something before the next meeting, have it done before the next meeting. If you say you are going to use a donation in a certain way, do it.

This requires planning on your part. Things don't just happen because you say they're going to happen. People make things happen.

A tool that I use to make sure things happen when I promise that they'll happen is a master calendar. I know—sounds really simple. And it is. And it works. It is worth my time investing in a little planning to make sure I achieve the outcomes I want.

I start by penciling in the due dates of the finished products—the proposal due dates, the gala, when I need the major gift to come in, for example. Then I work backwards with smaller steps.

- ◆ When do I have to have the first draft of the proposal written?
- ◆ When do I need material from my program and accounting staff?

◆ When do they need to review my budgets and program plans?

◆ When do I need that letter of commitment from my collaborators?

◆ When do I need the ad journal printed?

◆ When, then, is the artwork due?

◆ How much lead time do I need to give my donors for the ad journal?

◆ When do I follow up on the ask?

Such planning is especially helpful in a small shop where you are juggling multiple asks from multiple constituencies in multiple ways. I know I need something to simplify the dizzying array of tasks that I need to get done. If I don't write the tasks down, I tend to forget something; then I'm in a rush trying to catch up. I don't like that. Or I don't meet my deadlines and don't generate enough revenue, which means my organization suffers and can't completely meet its mission, which means the people my organization supports suffer. Outcomes like these are unacceptable.

If you want people to trust you and believe in what you say, you must follow through. Whatever tools you use to organize your activities are worth it. Follow-through is crucial. It is crucial on a personal level for people to trust you and at an

> **practical tip**
>
> I actually outline the specific tasks involved in achieving each separate project. Then I assign due dates to those tasks. Each project gets its own "task analysis." Then I combine all the due dates in a master task analysis, laid out in my annual calendar. This way, I know what I have to do when in order to meet my multiple priorities. And nothing slips through the cracks.
>
> Having everything written down helps me know how much I need to do in what period of time. This helps me to manage my time and workload. In addition, seeing a written schedule of activities helps me know what I can and cannot accomplish in any specific time frame so that I don't overpromise on what I can do.

organizational level for people to believe in your agency. It is branding in action. You need a good brand to attract your partners in the first place. You need to maintain that brand to keep your partners happy. I can't say it enough—follow through, follow through, follow through.

**Periodically Reassess Your Costs and Benefits**

Things don't always work out the way you want them or expect them to. Sometimes it takes you longer to implement a project than you thought it would. Sometimes circumstances change. Sometimes you made an assumption that turned out not to be true. A host of things can happen to change the calculations of the costs and benefits associated with a particular partnership.

Because things change, you need to periodically reassess your cost-benefit analyses. If the project is taking longer than you expected to implement, for example, you probably have higher staffing costs associated with the wait or you miscalculated how long it would take you to hire program personnel. Here are some criteria to keep in mind:

- If you are experiencing higher costs due to the delay, is the project still feasible or do you need to walk away?

- If there is a delay in project implementation, will you still be able to meet your partners' needs when you promised or do you need to renegotiate the terms of the partnership?

- If market conditions have changed, what impact does that have on your results?

- What about your partners' results?

- Will your revenues still be equal to or outweigh your expenses?

- Will you still be able to realize the return on investment you thought you would?

- Will you still be able to meet cash-flow needs?

I talked about financial considerations in **Chapter Six** and ensuring maximum profit in **Chapter Seven**. Run those analyses whenever there are changes to your inputs or your external environment. The world is constantly changing. Make sure you keep the benefits of your partnerships intact as you experience those changes.

Report back to your partners about the success of the investments they've made to your mission. Communicate to them regularly the status of that investment. Continue to use good communication and relationship-building skills. Use a planning tool to make sure that you follow through on your promises. And periodically reassess the costs and benefits of a partnership over time.

## To Recap

- ◆ Report progress on meeting mission-related needs back to contributors.

- ◆ Use your communication and relationship-building skills to maintain the partnership as the environment changes.

- ◆ Always follow through on your promises.

- ◆ Periodically run your financial analyses to make sure your benefits still outweigh your costs.

# Conclusion

## Wrapping It All Up

Well, we are at the end of the book. I've defined partners as being any persons or groups that interact with your agency and are interested in promoting its success. Defining partnerships broadly can lead to rewards beyond just money, rewards that are equally as important to your agency as money. I have talked about identifying partners through your organization's strategic plan and existing partnership base, exploring partnerships with organizations with shared goals, and pursuing partnerships with organizations with shared markets. I talked about the utilization of good communication and relationship-building skills. I wove throughout the conversation how important it is to understand your partners' needs and values if you are to structure a win-win partnership. I covered how different types of contributions can improve your bottom line and practices for accepting and receipting them.

I also talked about revenues and expenses, direct and indirect costs, opportunity costs, and pricing strategies. I talked about total costs and their effect on net income. I then covered how to calculate return on investment and how to use that information in deciding which partnerships to pursue and which not to. Calculating profit margin tells us where we realize the most efficient use of resources. Finally, to be successful, we must take into account cash flow and cash-flow considerations.

I then turned our attention to the factors that go into actually making the deal and having it come to fruition. I talked about fair process, fair outcomes, ethics, and when to walk away. Finally, I turned our attention to maintaining the partnership once it is formed.

## Conclusion

These are the tools I use to build up my partnership base, increase my organizational capacity, and improve my organization's effectiveness, both in terms of service delivery and market positioning. I am a successful fundraiser, in large part due to my ability to form and maintain partnerships. I hope that you and your organization, by developing your partnership base, raise lots of money and build a solid future.

# Appendix A

# Association of Fundraising Professionals Code of Ethical Principles and Standards

## ETHICAL PRINCIPLES • Adopted 1964; amended Sept. 2007

The Association of Fundraising Professionals (AFP) exists to foster the development and growth of fundraising professionals and the profession, to promote high ethical behavior in the fundraising profession, and to preserve and enhance philanthropy and volunteerism. Members of AFP are motivated by an inner drive to improve the quality of life through the causes they serve. They serve the ideal of philanthropy, are committed to the preservation and enhancement of volunteerism, and hold stewardship of these concepts as the overriding direction of their professional life. They recognize their responsibility to ensure that needed resources are vigorously and ethically sought and that the intent of the donor is honestly fulfilled. To these ends, AFP members, both individual and business, embrace certain values that they strive to uphold in performing their responsibilities for generating philanthropic support. AFP business members strive to promote and protect the work and mission of their client organizations.

AFP members both individual and business aspire to:

- ◆ practice their profession with integrity, honesty, truthfulness and adherence to the absolute obligation to safeguard the public trust
- ◆ act according to the highest goals and visions of their organizations, professions, clients, and consciences

- put philanthropic mission above personal gain
- inspire others through their own sense of dedication and high purpose
- improve their professional knowledge and skills, so that their performance will better serve others
- demonstrate concern for the interests and well-being of individuals affected by their actions
- value the privacy, freedom of choice, and interests of all those affected by their actions
- foster cultural diversity and pluralistic values and treat all people with dignity and respect
- affirm, through personal giving, a commitment to philanthropy and its role in society
- adhere to the spirit as well as the letter of all applicable laws and regulations
- advocate within their organizations adherence to all applicable laws and regulations
- avoid even the appearance of any criminal offense or professional misconduct
- bring credit to the fundraising profession by their public demeanor
- encourage colleagues to embrace and practice these ethical principles and standards
- be aware of the codes of ethics promulgated by other professional organizations that serve philanthropy

## ETHICAL STANDARDS

Furthermore, while striving to act according to the above values, AFP members, both individual and business, agree to abide (and to ensure, to the best of their ability, that all members of their staff abide) by the

AFP standards. Violation of the standards may subject the member to disciplinary sanctions, including expulsion, as provided in the AFP Ethics Enforcement Procedures.

## MEMBER OBLIGATIONS

1. Members shall not engage in activities that harm the members' organizations, clients, or profession.

2. Members shall not engage in activities that conflict with their fiduciary, ethical, and legal obligations to their organizations, clients, or profession.

3. Members shall effectively disclose all potential and actual conflicts of interest; such disclosure does not preclude or imply ethical impropriety.

4. Members shall not exploit any relationship with a donor, prospect, volunteer, client, or employee for the benefit of the members or the members' organizations.

5. Members shall comply with all applicable local, state, provincial and federal civil and criminal laws.

6. Members recognize their individual boundaries of competence and are forthcoming and truthful about their professional experience and qualifications and will represent their achievements accurately and without exaggeration.

7. Members shall present and supply products and/or services honestly and without misrepresentation and will clearly identify the details of those products, such as availability of the products and/or services and other factors that may affect the suitability of the products and/or services for donors, clients, or nonprofit organizations.

8. Members shall establish the nature and purpose of any contractual relationship at the outset and will be responsive and available to organizations and their employing organizations before, during, and after any sale of materials and/or services. Members will comply with all fair and reasonable obligations created by the contract.

9. Members shall refrain from knowingly infringing the intellectual property rights of other parties at all times. Members shall address and rectify any inadvertent infringement that may occur.

10. Members shall protect the confidentiality of all privileged information relating to the provider/client relationships.

11. Members shall refrain from any activity designed to disparage competitors untruthfully.

**SOLICITATION AND USE OF PHILANTHROPIC FUNDS**

12. Members shall take care to ensure that all solicitation and communication materials are accurate and correctly reflect their organizations' mission and use of solicited funds.

13. Members shall take care to ensure that donors receive informed, accurate, and ethical advice about the value and tax implications of contributions.

14. Members shall take care to ensure that contributions are used in accordance with donors' intentions.

15. Members shall take care to ensure proper stewardship of all revenue sources, including timely reports on the use and management of such funds.

16. Members shall obtain explicit consent by donors before altering the conditions of financial transactions.

**PRESENTATION OF INFORMATION**

17. Members shall not disclose privileged or confidential information to unauthorized parties.

18. Members shall adhere to the principle that all donor and prospect information created by, or on behalf of, an organization or a client is the property of that organization or client and shall not be transferred or utilized except on behalf of that organization or client.

19. Members shall give donors and clients the opportunity to have their names removed from lists that are sold to, rented to, or exchanged with other organizations.

20. Members shall, when stating fundraising results, use accurate and consistent accounting methods that conform to the appropriate guidelines adopted by the American Institute of Certified Public Accountants (AICPA)* for the type of organization involved. (* In countries outside of the United States, comparable authority should be utilized.)

## COMPENSATION AND CONTRACTS

21. Members shall not accept compensation or enter into a contract that is based on a percentage of contributions; nor shall members accept finder's fees or contingent fees. Business members must refrain from receiving compensation from third parties derived from products or services for a client without disclosing that third-party compensation to the client (for example, volume rebates from vendors to business members).

22. Members may accept performance-based compensation, such as bonuses, provided such bonuses are in accord with prevailing practices within the members' own organizations and are not based on a percentage of contributions.

23. Members shall neither offer nor accept payments or special considerations for the purpose of influencing the selection of products or services.

24. Members shall not pay finder's fees, commissions, or percentage compensation based on contributions, and shall take care to discourage their organizations from making such payments.

25. Any member receiving funds on behalf of a donor or client must meet the legal requirements for the disbursement of those funds. Any interest or income earned on the funds should be fully disclosed.

# Appendix B

## Grant Professionals Association Code of Ethics

Revised 10/5/11

The Grant Professionals Association (GPA), a nonprofit membership association, is committed to serving the greater public good by practicing the highest ethical and professional standards. Ethics refer to the rules or standards governing the conduct of a person or members of a profession.

Members have joined forces to be the leading authority and resource for the practice of grantsmanship in all sectors of the field. Membership in this association promotes positive relationships between grant professionals and their stakeholders, provides a vehicle for grant professionals to gain professional growth and development, and enhances the public image and recognition of the profession within the greater philanthropic, public, and private funding communities. Members' foundation is stimulated by the rich diversity within the grant profession.

Members, among other things, are to:

- practice their profession with the highest sense of integrity, honesty, and truthfulness to maintain and broaden public confidence
- to all applicable laws and regulations in all aspects of grantsmanship
- continually improve their professional knowledge and skills

- promote positive relationships between grant professionals and their stakeholders

- value the privacy, freedom, choice, and interests of all those affected by their actions

- ensure that funds are solicited according to program guidelines

- to acceptable means of compensation for services performed; pro bono work is encouraged

- foster cultural diversity and pluralistic values and treat all people with dignity and respect

- become leaders and role models in the field of grantsmanship

- encourage colleagues to embrace and practice GPA's Code of Ethics and Standards of Professional Practice.

**Standards of Professional Practice**

As members, respect and honor the above principles and guidelines established by the GPA Code of Ethics, any infringement or breach of standards outlined in the Code are subject to disciplinary sanctions, including expulsion, to be determined by a committee elected by their peers.

**Professional Obligations**

1. Members shall act according to the highest ethical standards of their institution, profession, and conscience.

2. Members shall obey all applicable local, state, provincial, and federal civil and criminal laws and regulations.

3. Members shall avoid the appearance of any criminal offense or professional misconduct.

4. Members shall disclose all relationships that might constitute, or appear to constitute, conflicts of interest.

5. Members shall not be associated directly or indirectly with any service, product, individuals, or organizations in a way that they know is misleading.

6. Members shall not abuse any relationship with a donor, prospect, volunteer or employee to the benefit of the member or the member's organization.

7. Members shall recognize their individual boundaries of competence and be forthcoming and truthful about their professional experience, knowledge, and expertise.

8. Members shall continually strive to improve their personal competence.

## Solicitation and Use of Funds

9. Members shall take care to ensure that all solicitation materials are accurate and correctly reflect the organization's mission and use of solicited funds.

10. Members shall take care to ensure that grants are used in accordance with the grant's intent.

## If Applicable

11. Members shall take care to ensure proper use of funds, including timely reports on the use and management of such funds.

12. Members shall obtain explicit consent by the grantor before altering the conditions of grant agreements.

## Presentation of Information

13. Members shall not disclose privileged information to unauthorized parties. Information acquired from consumers is confidential. This includes verbal and written disclosures, records, and video or audio recording of an activity or presentation without appropriate releases.

14. Members shall not plagiarize in any professional work, including, but not limited to grant proposals, journal articles/magazines, scholarly works, advertising/marketing materials, websites, scientific articles, self-plagiarism, etc.

15. Members are responsible for knowing the confidentiality regulations within their jurisdiction.

16. Members shall use accurate and consistent accounting methods that conform to the appropriate guidelines adopted by the American Institute of Certified Public Accountants (AICPA) for the type of organization involved. (In countries outside of the United States, comparable authority should be utilized).

**Compensation**

17. Members shall work for a salary or fee.

18. Members may accept performance-based compensation, such as bonuses, provided such bonuses are in accordance with prevailing practices within the members' own organizations and are not based on a percentage of grant monies.

19. Members shall not accept or pay a finder's fee, commission, or percentage compensation based on grants and shall take care to discourage their organizations from making such payments.

20. Compensation should not be written into grants unless allowed by the funder.

# Appendix C

# Glossary

**990:** Tax returns of tax-exempt organizations.

**990-PF:** Tax return of foundations.

**Active listening:** Listening technique that involves use of the feedback loop.

**Brand:** Reputation; how an organization is known in the community.

**Brand value:** Monetary or financial worth of an organization's reputation.

**Cause marketing:** A partnership between a nonprofit and for-profit designed to increase the for-profit's market share or exposure by financially supporting the nonprofit's cause.

**Corporate culture:** The expressed and unexpressed codes of behavior in different organizational settings.

**Decode:** How a message is understood by the receiver.

**Encode:** How a message is delivered by the messenger.

**Feedback loop:** The communication loop created when one person delivers a message and the other paraphrases what they heard.

**Fringe benefits:** Compensation provided to employees that is not attributable to salary and wages.

**Full-time equivalent (FTE):** The number of total hours worked in one week divided by the number of compensated hours in a full-time work week. The percentage time employees work in one position. A partial FTE works less than full-time in one position whereas more than one FTE has two or more people working in the same position.

**General and administrative expenses (G&A):** Expenses that are incurred in the overall operation of an agency that are not directly attributable to one program or event. Also known as overhead expenses and indirect expenses.

**Gross revenue:** The total income before expenses are deducted. Also known as gross income.

**In-kind contributions:** Noncash donations.

**Indirect costs:** Costs not directly attributable to one specific program or event. Also known as general and administrative expenses or overhead expenses.

**Logo:** A visual representation of a brand.

**Market potential:** Unmet demand.

**Market share:** The percentage of the total need that one group meets.

**Market-based pricing:** A pricing strategy whereby price is determined by what similar organizations are charging for similar goods and services.

**Mission:** The purpose of an organization.

**Mission-related investment:** A hybrid form of charitable giving incorporating aspects of both a loan and a grant. Also sometimes referred to as a program-related investment.

**Net revenues:** Income after expenses. Net income.

**Noise:** The external distractions that surround a message being received.

**Operating expenses:** Costs attributable to the operation of a program or organization.

**Operationalize:** To make a part of organizational operations. The design of processes and procedures to implement goals and objectives.

**Opportunity costs:** The costs associated with choosing one alternative over another.

**Organizational capacity:** An organization's ability to meet its goals and objectives.

**Overarching goals:** Goals that supersede each parties' interests.

**Overhead:** Expenses that are incurred in the overall operation of an agency that are not directly attributable to one program or event. Also known as general and administrative expenses (G&A) and indirect expenses.

**Partner:** A person or organization that contributes to the overall success of your organization.

**Partnership:** An agreement between two or more people or organizations whereby all partners receive something of value.

**Profit:** Excess revenues after expenses. Also known as net income.

**Profit margin:** Net income divided by total revenues. Profit margin tells you the percentage of total revenues that are used up in producing the good or service and how much is profit.

**Profit-based pricing:** A pricing strategy where price is determined by cost plus desired profit.

**Restricted income:** Income to be used only for purposes designated by the donor or funder. Income that is restricted for specific uses.

**Return on investment (ROI):** Net income divided by total expenses. Return on investment tells you how leveraged your costs are, i.e., how much income is realized by incurring costs in a certain way.

**Revenue:** Income.

**Revenue mix:** The mix of activities an organization undertakes to meet its income goals.

**Revenue structure:** The overall structure of an organization's revenue streams. The organization's revenue mix.

**Shot-gunning:** Submitting the same proposal to different funders.

**Strategic plan:** The overall plan outlining the goals of an organization for the next 3-5 years and the strategies the organization will use to meet those goals.

**Unrestricted income:** Contributions that are not designated for use in a certain way.

# Appendix D

# Recommended Reading

Andresen, Katya. 2006. *Robin Hood Marketing: Stealing Corporate Savvy to Sell Just Causes.* San Francisco, CA: Jossey-Bass.

Barbato, Joseph. 2005. *Attracting the Attention Your Cause Deserves.* Medfield, MA: Emerson and Church.

Bell, Jean, Jan Masaoka, and Steve Zimmerman. 2010. *Nonprofit Sustainability: Making Strategic Decisions for Financial Viability.* San Francisco, CA: Jossey-Bass.

Connor, Tracy D, editor. 2011. *The Volunteer Management Handbook: Leadership Strategies for Success* (Second Edition). Hoboken, NJ: John Wiley & Sons Inc.

Crutchfield, Leslie R. and Heather McLeod Grant. 2007. *Forces for Good: The Six Practices of High-Impact Nonprofits.* San Francisco, CA: Jossey-Bass.

Daw, Jocelyne. 2006. *Cause Marketing for Nonprofits: Partner for Purpose, Passion and Profits.* Hoboken, NJ: John Wiley & Sons Inc.

Durham, Sarah. 2010. *Brandraising: How Nonprofits Raise Visibility and Money Through Smart Communications.* San Francisco, CA: Jossey-Bass.

Eisenstein, Amy M. 2010. *50 Asks in 50 Weeks: A Guide to Better Fundraising for Your Small Development Shop.* Rancho Santa Margarita, CA: CharityChannel Press.

Grace, Kay Sprinkel. 2007. *Fundraising Mistakes that Bedevil All Boards (And Staff Too): a 1-hour Guide to Identifying and Overcoming Obstacles to Your Success*. Medfield, MA: Emerson and Church.

Landsdowne, David. 2004. *The Relentlessly Practical Guide to Raising Serious Money: Proven Strategies for Nonprofit Organizations*. Medfield, MA: Emerson and Church.

Lysakowski, Linda. 2011. *Capital Campaigns: Everything You NEED to Know*. Rancho Santa Margarita, CA: CharityChannel Press.

Lysakowski, Linda. 2012. *Fundraising for the GENIUS*. Rancho Santa Margarita, CA: for the Genius Press.

Lysakowski, Linda. 2012. *Raise More Money from Your Business Community: A Practical Guide for Tapping into Corporate Charitable Giving*. Rancho Santa Margarita, CA: CharityChannel Press.

Lysakowski, Linda. 2006. *Recruiting and Training Fundraising Volunteers*. Hoboken, NJ: John Wiley & Sons Inc.

Lysakowski, Linda. 2007. *Nonprofit Essentials: The Development Plan*. Hoboken, NJ: John Wiley & Sons Inc.

Martin, Patricia. 2004. *Made Possible By: Succeeding with Sponsorship*. San Francisco, CA: Jossey-Bass.

McLaughlin, Thomas A. 2006. *Nonprofit Strategic Positioning: Decide Where to Be, Plan What to Do*. Hoboken, NJ: John Wiley & Sons Inc.

McLaughlin, Thomas A. 2009. *Streetsmart Financial Basics for Nonprofit Managers*. Hoboken, NJ: John Wiley & Sons.

Olshansky, Norman and Linda Lysakowski, editors. 2011. *You and Your Nonprofit: Practical Advice and Tips from the CharityChannel Community*. Rancho Santa Margarita, CA: CharityChannel Press.

Oppelt, Joanne. 2011. *Confessions of a Successful Grants Writer: A Complete Guide to Discovering and Obtaining Funding*. Rancho Santa Margarita, CA: CharityChannel Press.

Oppelt, Joanne. 2013. *Succeed in Your Nonprofit Funding Partnerships: Analyzing Their Costs and Benefits.* Rancho Santa Margarita, CA: CharityChannel Press.

Panas, Jerold. 2006-2007. *Asking: A 59-Minute Guide to Everything Board Members, Volunteers, and Staff Must Know to Secure the Gift.* Medfield, MA: Emerson and Church.

Stroman, M. Kent. 2011. *Asking About Asking: Mastering the Art of Conversational Fundraising.* Rancho Santa Margarita, CA: CharityChannel Press.

Teitel, Martin. 2006. *"Thank You for Submitting Your Proposal": A Foundation Director Reveals What Happens Next.* Medfield, MA: Emerson and Church.

# Index

## A

**accounts, chart of**, 71, 73
**assets**, 48
**Association of Fundraising Professionals (AFP)**, 121
　Ethical Principles, 121–22
**audits**, 48

## B

**brand**, 6, 8, 27, 33–35, 37, 53, 56–57, 61, 67, 81, 92, 116, 131–32
　value, 131
**branding**, 34, 46, 48, 105–6, 116
**budget**, 21, 45, 51, 60, 72, 74–76, 80–82, 87–88, 104, 115
　direct cost, sample, 73, 75

## C

**capacity**, 32, 48, 51, 61–62, 120, 133
**cash flow**, 51, 93–94, 96–97
**cash-flow**, 47
**cause marketing**, 14, 34, 135
**CharityChannel Press**, 135–37
**clients**, 9–10, 12–15, 33, 35, 40, 51, 56, 59, 61, 63–64, 105, 121, 123–25
**Code of Ethics, Grant Professionals Association**, 107, 127, 129
**constituents**, 3, 8, 13–14, 29, 50, 56, 61, 64–65, 67, 81, 105
**corporate culture**, 18, 55–56, 58, 69, 131
**costs**, 21, 24, 32, 35–36, 60–61, 67–68, 71–73, 76–77, 80–86, 88–89, 92–93, 96–97, 104, 108, 112, 116–17, 119, 132–33, 137
　business, 36–37
　direct, 72–73, 76–77, 80
　indirect, 72, 77–78, 80, 88, 119, 132
　marketing, 31
　opportunity, 80–81, 133
　personnel, 74
　program, 60, 72
　staffing, 116
**culture**, 5, 14, 17–18, 55, 57–59, 68, 100

clash, 57
organizational, 99
organization's, 57
values, 55
**customer bases**, 7–8, 13, 35–37

## D

**decoding**, 18–19
**direct cost budget, sample**, 73, 75
**donations**, 4, 8, 25, 30, 33, 35, 41–42, 64, 68, 93, 102, 119, 124–25, 134
  cash, 27–28, 36
  in-kind, 8, 27, 29–32, 36, 90, 132
  noncash, 29
**donors**
  corporate, 87
  current, 9, 24, 112
  high-maintenance, 81
  individual, 84
  keeping, 24
  long-time, 112
  loyal, 34
  third-party, 35
**donor strategies**, 29

## E

**encoding**, 18–19
**ethics**, 107, 119, 121–22, 127–29
**exit strategy**, 108–9
**expenses**, 28, 33–34, 36, 45, 47, 62, 72–80, 83–86, 89, 91–96, 112, 116, 119, 132–33
  administrative, 61, 132–33
  direct, 72, 76–77, 80
  general and administrative (G&A), 78, 132–33
  indirect, 132–33
  nonpersonnel, 74, 76, 79
  operating, 4, 32, 96, 132
  overhead, 28, 77–78, 80, 132
  personnel, 73–76, 78–79
  staff support, 112
  total, 71–72, 74, 76, 79–80, 84–87, 90–92, 95, 119, 133

## F

**feedback**, 22, 25, 32, 40
  feedback loop, 17, 19–20, 25, 58, 102, 114, 131
**fringe benefits**, 73, 75, 77–78, 80, 131
**FTE (full-time equivalent)**, 74–75, 77–78, 80, 132
**funding partnerships**, 41, 50, 66, 71, 81, 85, 91, 97, 103, 105, 111

## G

**Grant Professionals Association (GPA)**, 127
  Code of Ethics, 107, 127, 129
  Standards of Professional Practice, 128

## I

**income**, 27, 29, 31, 33, 35–37, 60, 89, 125, 132–33
  net, 36, 47, 71, 80, 83–92, 94–96, 119, 132–33
**in-kind donations**, 8, 27, 29–32, 36, 90, 132

# Index

**investment, mission-related**, 96, 132

## L

**liabilities**, 47–48, 73

## M

**market**, 4, 7–8, 13, 34–35, 42, 46, 48–49, 64, 66, 69, 83–84, 86, 132
  positioning, 48, 120
  share, 48–49, 57, 132
  strategy, 37
  unmet demand, 35, 49, 132
**market-based pricing**, 83, 85, 132
**mission**, 10, 57
**mission-related investment**, 96, 132

## N

**net income**, 36, 47, 71, 80, 83–92, 94–96, 119, 132–33

## O

**operating expenses**, 4, 32, 96, 132
**opportunity costs**, 80–81, 133
**organizational capacity**, 32, 48, 51, 61–62, 120, 133
**overhead, rate**, 77–80

## P

**partners**
  business, 49
  community, 14
  defined, 119
  existing, 3
  financial, 29
  funding, 14, 53, 112
  potential, 2, 3, 9, 11, 15, 17, 19, 20–22, 24, 39–41, 43–45, 47–49, 51, 53, 58, 99–100, 105
**partnership**
  agreements, 55, 65, 108
  base, 119–20
  cause-marketing, 8
  defining, 119
  existing, 3, 113
  formation, 97
  fundraising, 41, 50, 71, 81, 91, 103
  long-term, 23, 36
  negotiations, 105, 107
  obligations, 66
  potential, 24, 55
  successful, 2–3, 50, 58
  win-win, 119
**pricing, market based**, 83, 85, 132
**pricing strategies**, 34, 71, 83, 88, 119, 132–33
**profit**, 89, 91, 93, 95, 97
**profit margin**, 47, 89, 92–93, 96–97, 133
**program costs**, 60, 72
**program-related investment**, 96, 132

## R

**return on investment**, 90–91

**revenue**, 5, 7–8, 25, 33–36, 42, 47, 50–52, 60–61, 68, 73, 76, 80, 83–87, 89–97, 115–16, 119, 133
  goals, 85
  sources, 75, 124
  strategies, 80, 87
  streams, 7, 13, 51, 85, 134
  structure, 85–87, 134
**revenue mix**, 29, 96, 133–34

## S

**staff**, 5, 23, 31–32, 34, 37, 42, 51–52, 60–61, 67, 69, 72, 74, 77, 81, 104, 112, 122, 136–37
  unpaid, 32, 62
**strategic plan**, 2–3, 12, 15, 64, 82–83, 100, 119, 134

## V

**vacancy rate**, 105–6
**values**
  common, 59, 100
  cultural, 55
  fulfillment, 104, 109
  proposition, 100
**volunteer**
  base, 7, 62, 65, 104
  time, 33, 90, 103, 112
  trainings, 7, 112
**volunteerism**, 121
**volunteers**, 4, 6, 9–14, 22–23, 25, 27, 31–34, 36–37, 41–42, 56, 61, 64, 90, 112, 123, 129, 137

If you enjoyed this book, you'll want to pick up the other books in the CharityChannel Press **In the Trenches™** series.

www.CharityChannel.com

In addition, there are dozens of titles currently moving to publication. So be sure to check the CharityChannel.com bookstore.

www.CharityChannel.com

**CharityChannel PRESS**

And now introducing **For the GENIUS® Press,** an imprint that produces books on just about any topic that people want to learn. You don't have to be a genius to read a **GENIUS** book, but you'll sure be smarter once you do!

# Fundraising for the GENIUS™

The only book you'll ever need to raise more money for your nonprofit organization.

FOR THE GENIUS IN ALL OF US™

Linda Lysakowski, ACFRE

www.ForTheGENIUS.com

**P R E S S**